Market or Die

A Down & Dirty Guide to Marketing Your Book

by

Jennifer Fusco

Bell Bridge Books

This is a work of fiction. Names, characters, places and incidents are either the products of the author's imagination or are used fictitiously. Any resemblance to actual persons (living or dead), events or locations is entirely coincidental.

Bell Bridge Books
PO BOX 300921
Memphis, TN 38130
Print ISBN: 978-1-61194-590-4

Bell Bridge Books is an Imprint of BelleBooks, Inc.

We at BelleBooks enjoy hearing from readers.
Visit our websites
BelleBooks.com
BellBridgeBooks.com
ImaJinnBooks.com

10 9 8 7 6 5 4 3 2 1

Cover design: Debra Dixon
Interior design: Hank Smith
Photo/Art credits:
Market or Die Logo @ Jennifer Fusco| Market or Die
Mark © Claudio Bertoloni | Dreamstime.com
Pen © Chuhail | Dreamstime.com

:Ldmj:01:

Dedication

As I grew up, my grandmother always told me I could be anything I wanted to be if I put my mind to it. And, she was right. During her elder years, our family lost her to dementia, and she never knew that I decided to pursue a writing career, was signed by an agent, or sold a book to a publisher. Our family lost her again during the writing of this book. She passed away at the age of ninety-two. Ann Adkins, this book is for you. I did it. I hope you are looking down on me with a heart filled with pride. Rest in peace.

Foreword

Everyone thinks their book should be a runaway bestseller. People will buy it, they'll read it, fall in love with it, and soon it will be made into a major motion picture starring Meryl Streep and Chris Hemsworth, and be directed by Martin Scorsese. It's a great thing to aspire to.

Sometimes things like this do happen: Harry Potter, *Twilight*, *Fifty Shades of Grey*. The buzz gets out there and, like magic, a bestseller emerges. But more often than not, it's hard work and perseverance that ultimately gives your book a fighting chance to become successful.

Authors need to use all of the tools at their disposal: their publisher, agent, friends, relatives, and readers. But how to do this effectively is the trick.

Jennifer Fusco has put together a comprehensive guide to creatively and productively market your book. Pulling from her experience and resources, Jennifer guides the reader through the maze of what to do before and after the book is written by offering options to finding readers and opening doors to new avenues for "getting yourself out there."

So, sit home and wonder why no one is buying your book, or read *Market or Die*. See that you are responsible for your own destiny by taking control of marketing your book, and discover how wonderful it feels to have all the power.

—*Barbara Vey*

As Contributing Editor for Publishers Weekly, *Barbara Vey brings readers and writers together with her popular Beyond Her Book blog. Recipient of the 2012 RWA Vivian Stephens Industry Award, 2013* Romantic Times *Melinda Helfer Fairy Godmother Award, and author of* Book Marketing, Book Trailers, and Author Etiquette in a Nutshell, *Barbara has become a sought-after speaker. From her entertaining "Drive-By Videos" to reader feedback on books with WW Ladies Book Club and Hot New Tuesday Releases, BHB continues to grow into a must-read daily adventure.*

Introduction

Authors agree. Marketing sucks. You don't have to explain why you feel overwhelmed at the mention of the word marketing. You're not alone. No author sets out to market a book—authors write. But, like it or not, marketing has become part of an author's career. In a recent conversation with urban fantasy author Anton Strout, he posed the question: "Is it that authors are overwhelmed by marketing, or are we just too focused on the writing?" After a bit of a debate, he said, "writers have to embrace marketing, even though they'd rather write." Anton continued by saying, "As the landscape of publishing changes, so are the responsibilities of the modern author. It's not a question of *if* you should, it's a question of *how* you should (market) now."

Luckily, you have *Market or Die: A Down & Dirty Guide to Marketing Your Book*.

But before we jump into the *how*, let's talk about *why* marketing is important to your career. Marketing is about building relationships. These relationships will generate demand for you and your work.

That's it. Plain and simple.

To create demand, effective marketing is split into two phases: strategy and execution. Some authors jump into the execution phase without taking the time to plan a strategy, then sit back and wonder why their plans failed. However, this won't be you. Why? Because, by the end of this book, you will have learned that marketing should be a coordinated, integrated effort. A cohesive plan will help you make sure all of your marketing efforts are "hitting" at exactly the same time. A one-time promotion, never to be seen or heard from again, won't do you any good . . . ever.

An integrated strategy should include plans for social media, advertising, in-person and online events, promotions, endorsements, press coverage, reviews, and word of mouth (word of mouth is often referred to as "buzz"). And all of it should include a soft-sell message designed to build a relationship with your readers. In this book, you will master the skills of soft-selling so that readers will feel emotionally invested in you. That emotional connection will translate into sales. You will learn how to compose a marketing plan, how to implement the strategies therein, and how to gauge the efficacy of your ventures. The tools contained in this book will enable you to market your book successfully.

So, are you with me?

Fantastic!

Let's get started.

x

Chapter One

Authors, Attitudes, and Marketing

The idea of selling a book is simple. You have a great story, an interesting title, a striking cover image, and enticing back cover copy. Your novel should sell itself, right? Wrong. Today, the market is inundated with books competing for readers' attention. It doesn't matter if the book is published traditionally or through independent channels, more and more of the weight of book publicity is being placed on the author's shoulders.

Authors are creative and fascinating people. They create worlds and characters; weave compelling conflict into stories; and craft edge-of-your-seat plotlines and moving dialogue. So, why do authors with such innate creativity shrink at the idea of marketing?

Some don't know where to start, while others don't give themselves enough credit for being good at book promotion. Marketing is a discipline that combines strategy, creativity, and execution. It is a skill easily learned and implemented.

Successful authors have understood and adopted marketing into their careers and recognize it is as important as the writing itself. *New York Times* bestselling romance author Lori Handeland says, "From the beginning of my career, I knew I needed to be more than just another author with a book to sell. I knew I needed to lay the groundwork to build relationships with my readers. I wanted to get to know my readers, and let them into my world as much as possible. Career longevity begins with the fans you make on your first sale, and those fans will be the ones who stay with you forever."

Fellow romance author, *New York Times* and *USA Today* bestseller Tawny Weber agrees. She says, "I began studying marketing, taking workshops, and asking promotional advice long before I had a contract for my first book, because I understood one simple fact. The authors who reached more readers sold more books. Since my goal has always been to have a successful, long-term career as an author, I knew marketing would be a vital tool to achieve that goal."

You, too, can achieve Ms. Handeland's and Ms. Weber's levels of success by accepting that marketing is a part of your job.

Success or failure in marketing depends on the effectiveness of your communication. Shouting the release of your new book from the rooftops will only be effective if those listening care. In marketing, it is essential to not only craft clear, concise messages, but also deliver those messages to the buying public who will deem your book to be of value.

It is also important to note that communication is a two-way street. When you find the subset of the buying public who enjoys your work, it is your responsibility to not only engage with them, but listen to their wants and needs.

For the book-buying public, authors are perceived to be superstars. Moviegoers may not be able to connect with their Hollywood idols in the way they may wish, but for readers, authors are real, attainable people they can connect with. Harnessing and fostering that connection leads to discoverability, and, once discovered, your fan base flourishes.

It is also important to examine why you should learn how to communicate effectively. Communication is the basis to selling a product. Effective communication is not about "you." It is about cultivating your readership and providing readers with the content they desire. Writer Matt Doss, author of *The Son of David*, says, "While we have ample opportunity to edit and rewrite our words during the editing process, we do not have that luxury when speaking. Getting people interested in our work means getting people interested in us. They know they can read our work, but they want to be inspired by and connected to the author. That spark of connectivity normally only comes from effective communication."

A clearly constructed marketing message can be written or spoken. To become successful at marketing, you must understand your end goal is to make a sale. In order to make a sale, it is important to learn how to communicate your marketing message effectively. Mixing effective messages with the intent to sell isn't a new concept.

In 1898, Elias St. Elmo Lewis, an advertising and sales innovator, crafted a communication model, later recorded in 1903, to explain personal selling. BusinessDictionary.com defines personal selling as face-to-face selling in which the seller attempts to persuade a buyer to make a purchase.

Lewis's model attempts to clarify how the seller can influence the buyer through messaging. Lewis's model was later published by CP Russell's "How to Write a Sales-Making Letter" in *Printers Ink* in 1921, and the four-layer model which is comprised of Awareness, Interest, Desire, and Action (AIDA), is still relevant today. Lewis and Russell's theory was used as a basic principle in advertising. However, today's marketing encompasses more than just traditional face-to-face selling and print advertising.

Every day, readers are bombarded with marketing messages and headlines designed to grab their attention. Each message must work extremely hard to get not only noticed, but acted upon by the buying public. Therefore, the importance of learning how to construct a marketing message designed to reach your intended reader is vital to career longevity. It is imperative to your career that you learn how to write with the intent to sell. When writing with the intent to sell, you will construct the most effective messages with a multi-phased approach.

Similar to creating advertising copy, pitching a book (with the intent to sell) to a reader can be accomplished in four simple sentences. These sentences are constructed as follows:

> **The Headline:** Attracts the reader.
>
> **The Sub-Line:** Relays the benefits of the book to the reader.
>
> **The Body:** Convinces the reader that this book will satisfy his or her needs.
>
> **The Call to Action:** Directs the reader toward the purchase of the book.

The idea sounds simple, and it is. The difficulty comes in writing an effective marketing message that incorporates each layer without sounding off-putting.

Below, you'll find a marketing message created for this book using the layered communication approach.

Are you happy with your current book sales? Would you like to learn how to market in order to increase your sales simply by building relationships? If you answered yes, Market or Die *can help. The simple act of building relationships using effective communication is covered in detail in Jennifer Fusco's latest book.*

Let's dissect the above paragraph to analyze how the reader is directed toward a purchase.

The headline is designed to grab the attention of the reader by asking a question. The sentence *Are you happy with your current book sales?* is written for the author who would answer "no," and thus continue to read further. The message is designed for the author who wants to increase sales.

The next sentence focuses on the benefits of the book. The sentence *Would you like to learn how to market in order to increase your sales simply by building relationships?* tells the reader what they will learn by reading the book.

Convincing the buyer this book will satisfy his or her needs is communicated in the sentence *If you answered yes,* Market or Die *can help.* This is the sentence which provides the solution to the reader's problem.

Leading the reader toward making a purchasing decision is implied in the last sentence—*The simple act of building relationships using effective communication is covered in detail in Jennifer Fusco's latest book.* This sentence invites the reader to buy the book in a non-threatening way.

The simplicity of a layered communication message allows it to be used as a checklist. It's impossible to sell anything without getting the buyer's attention. To write an effective headline, it is best to begin your message with wording that pulls your audience toward you. One of the ways to achieve this is to open with a question, such as:

Do you like . . . ?

Are you looking for . . . ?

Have you ever . . . ?

Do you think . . . ?

Although opening with a question isn't required, you may find it useful to begin with a question as you first develop your message. You can always refine the sentence and take out the question in later revisions. Using your title or describing a situation are alternative eye-catching openers and ways to begin your message.

You may start by asking yourself what it is about your book that captures a reader's attention. Or answer the question, why should your reader care? The rest of your message should be designed to keep the reader's concentration and sustain the reader's interest to learn more.

In nonfiction, grab the reader by telling him the crux of your topic. If you are writing fiction, tell the reader what's at stake in the story.

Other important tips:

* Avoid the use of the word "I" in your opening statement. In other words, refrain from the use of openers such as, "I think you'd like . . ." or "I've got a story you may . . ." Using the word "I" presses your opinion onto others. Remember, in order to become attractive to a buyer, it's important to pull a person in. Without a buyer, you cannot make a sale.

* Refrain from using words like "hot" or "best." They've become overused and lost their impact.

* Once your opening statement has an interested audience, you'll need to sustain their attention. To do this, you must state the benefit of what you have to offer. In the sub-line, focus on the book's benefits. If you need help cultivating the benefits, consider the following:

   * Address a problem facing your reader.

   * Offer a suggestion for a topic the reader finds interesting.

   * Focus on the theme or issues in the book.

   * Answer how the book will improve the reader's life.

Get to the point. Avoid boring the reader by using too many words. Prospective buyers are won and lost when they're forced to consider how the book will benefit them. State the benefits clearly. For fiction, this is the place to address the emotional conflict of the story.

The sub-line and body complement each other. So, as you begin writing the body, deliver the reason why you believe this book will satisfy your reader. If the reader has stuck with your message thus far, you have captured his or her interest. In the sentence that is the body, be sure to:

* Ensure your reader understands what your book offers.

* Tell your reader what makes your book desirable.

* Focus on the needs and wants of your reader.

* Create the motivation for buying the book.

If you are writing nonfiction, provide the answer to your reader's problem. It is vital that you summarize the reader's problem first, and then address how it will be solved. For fiction, this is where you place your story's hook. If the hook is expertly crafted, your readers will become so invested that they are compelled to read further.

The last—and most important—sentence is where you ask for the purchase. Here, the audience is directed toward buying the book with a buy link or learning opportunity, such as a website address. It is perfectly acceptable to ask someone to visit your website and then provide your web address. Also, if there are any time-sensitive messages, such as *On Sale Now*, or *For a Limited Time*, they would go in the call to action. You may also end your message by listing specific retailers where your work can be found.

Good communication will engage an audience, hook readers, and drive them toward an action. Learning how to communicate effectively is not buyer manipulation. It is simply providing a solution to a reader's need (sometimes before the reader realizes the need). When you reach readers who are interested in your work and perceive your content is of value, they will engage with you. This interaction can lead to a purchase. If they are satisfied with the content you provided, they will continue to engage with you long-term. Before you put together the marketing messages regarding your book, consider:

* How you will make readers aware of your book release.

* Your outreach strategy.

* What social media platforms you will use.

* What you want your reader to know about your book.

* How your book is made available to the public.

* What makes your book desirable?

* What benefit does your book offer the reader?

* How will you best interact with your readership?
* Do you feel comfortable asking for a purchase?
* How will you go about inviting the reader to buy your work?

Answering the above will help you craft your marketing messages. Then, once they are created, you need to answer the question of how and where will you use this type of communication and, more importantly, what actions will you take to support it?

Just as effective communication is layered, actions to take in order to apply your message are also multi-phased. There are many techniques available to help promote your message. Use these techniques to accompany each phase of your message. For example:

* To increase awareness about your book, put effort into outreach. Increase the rate and frequency of your participation on social media. Facebook and Twitter are two social media platforms which can assist you in spreading your marketing message.

* Gain attention for your book by communicating your marketing message to other authors who will help you find your audience by introducing you to their own.

* Newsletters are an effective method of communicating benefits to your readership. Send out a newsletter and include your marketing message.

* Communicate how your book satisfies the reader's needs by participating in book signings. Or, if in-person signings are not possible, schedule an event online.

* Support your call to action by ensuring your website is up to date and easily found. Provide a list or a link on your website to all the retail outlets where your book may be purchased.

In conclusion, crafting a marketing message is integral to the sales process. Not only does it promote discoverability, but it promotes the sale itself. In today's publishing landscape, the author has more control than ever before. Creating a marketing message and writing it with the intent to sell places the author in a position of power. Now, you have the ability to identify the reader who is most likely to make a purchase, rather than communicating a message with the hope it reaches someone who cares.

Today, you have the ability to not only create the work, but create the value of the work to the reader. This perceived value lends itself to career longevity, now and for years to come.

Key takeaways from this chapter:

* Marketing is a discipline that combines strategy, creativity, and execution. Mastery in marketing will come over time. Practice is key.

* Success or failure in marketing depends on the effectiveness of your communication. It is important that you communicate your message to an audience who cares.

* Once you find a subset of the buying public interested in your work, it is your responsibility to not only engage with them, but listen to their wants and needs. Engagement is essential to marketing success.

* Learning how to construct a marketing message, designed with your intended reader in mind, is vital to career longevity.

* Crafting a clear, succinct marketing message is similar to creating advertising copy. Use a four-layered approach: the headline, the sub-line, the body, and the call to action.

* In the body of the message, ensure the reader understands what the book offers, tell the reader what makes the book desirable, focus on the wants and needs of the reader, and create motivation for purchasing the book.

* Consider how you will make the reader aware of the book's release, your outreach strategy, what social media platforms you intend to use, what you want the reader to know about the story, how you will make the book available to the public, what makes the book desirable, what benefit the book offers the reader, if you feel comfortable asking for (or implying) a purchase, and how you will go about inviting the reader to buy the work.

Chapter Two

Developing a Target Audience and the Importance of Soft-Selling

When you sit down in front of the television and a commercial appears, some products interest you while others don't.

Have you ever asked yourself why?

Is it because the uninteresting products aren't designed for you? Or, maybe, you don't have a need for what the advertiser is trying to sell. Matching product to buyer isn't easy, and companies spend millions to find the right balance. You may not have millions to sink into marketing, but you can begin to market like a professional by using a marketing strategy to find your target audience. A target audience is a subset of the buying public who will deem your product or service worthy of purchase.

While finding such an audience sounds easy, it's not.

In order to find the group who will find your book worth buying, you must decide upon which marketing strategy you will use to uncover them. The four most basic types of marketing strategies are: Mass Marketing, Differentiated Marketing, Concentrated Marketing, and Niche Marketing.

Below is a further explanation of each strategy:

Mass Marketing

In Mass Marketing, it's assumed the product will appeal to everyone. Mass Marketing makes no distinctions between who will like the product and who will not. For Mass Marketing to be successful, you must have a recognizable brand and wide distribution. It is a passive form of marketing, similar to the cliché "throwing spaghetti at the wall and seeing what sticks."

Examples of authors who have wide recognizable brand recognition, large enough for successful mass marketing, are: Stephen King, Charlaine Harris, Stephenie Meyer, Nora Roberts, Lee Child, and George R.R. Martin. Mass marketing works best when you need nothing more to rely on selling the book other than your name and the book itself. Mass marketing can work for both fiction and nonfiction.

Differentiated Marketing

In Differentiated Marketing, the same product is marketed differently to different target consumers, depending on their interests and needs. Differentiated marketing anticipates the needs of varied audiences and plays into that need. For example, if you are marketing a car, you'd use different selling points for women than you would for men. Marketers may appeal to women's concern for safety, reliability, and comfort, where they may entice their target audience of men with the same car's gas mileage, horsepower, or low maintenance costs.

One example of how you may choose to use a differentiated strategy is by looking at the buying market as four separate buying groups. They are:

* Libraries
* Booksellers
* Readers
* Authors

In a differentiated strategy, you would find your target audience using a different "positioning statement" for each group. A positioning statement is a series of sentences which convey the unique value of the book to each buying group. Craft a positioning statement for each group by defining what makes your book stand out for the particular buying group.

Again, in differentiated marketing, to find a target audience among each group, the communication will be unique. Below are the positioning statements for *Market or Die* aimed at different buying groups.

* Libraries. *Based on fact and research*, Market or Die *is a useful reference book filled with timely instructions on book publicity which will not age.*

* Booksellers. *Nonfiction books continue to sell strongly in today's changing publishing world. Publisher's Weekly* reported in 2012, "(a) less severe decline in nonfiction sales was due in part to a drop of less than 1% in units, and while e-book sales rose 136.4%, to $468.2 million, the declines in the major print formats were much smaller compared to fiction." (Jim Milliot, "Industry Sales Pegged at $27.2 Billion," *Publisher's Weekly*, July 2012. Web, May 18, 2012)

* Readers. *While* Market or Die *is specifically written for authors, any reader looking to learn more about marketing can benefit.*

* Authors. Market or Die *is designed to instruct the author how to market their book and themselves by starting with a blank page and ending with a complete, measureable marketing plan.*

For fiction, a differentiated strategy may look like this:

* Libraries. The book has received special recognition in *Kirkus, Library Journal,* or *Romantic Times.*

* Booksellers. The book or author has received awards or an accolade for this book (e.g., Amazon Top 100 Author ranking). The author's previous books sold over "X" copies.

* Readers. This is where the marketing message created in Chapter One is used.

* Authors. This book is an excellent example of—fill in the blank (Point of View, Setting, Character, World Building)—and should be read by fellow authors as a learning tool.

The crux of a differentiated marketing plan is that the author can "argue" the multiple benefits of their book to find their target audience. A differentiated marketing plan can be used to market nonfiction or fiction.

Concentrated Marketing

In Concentrated Marketing, this is where all of your efforts are focused on a select group of people. Concentrated marketing is usually geared for smaller groups because the product is designed to appeal to a particular segment of the market. For example, a romance author marketing to romance readers is a form of concentrated marketing.

As authors are taking more control over their marketing, most are starting by executing a concentrated marketing plan focused solely on attracting one specific type of reader. A downside to concentrated marketing is that it can quickly lead to market saturation.

Niche Marketing

In Niche Marketing, the product is marketed to a specific group. Persons outside this group would have no interest in the product. Books of specificity are niche-marketed. For example, most cookbooks are mass-marketed, but Paleo cookbooks are marketed specifically to those interested in a healthy, whole foods, Paleo lifestyle. This book, *Market or Die*, is marketed using a niche strategy because it appeals only to authors. It is doubtful anyone outside the writing community would have a need for a book about book marketing.

The listing below includes the practical definition, the pros and cons, and the suggested marketing tools for each strategy.

Mass Marketing

Practical definition

In mass marketing, it is assumed that the book will appeal to an extremely large audience.

Pros

* Largest population reach.
* Works best if the book is for "everyone."
* Works best for books that readers need.

Cons

* Must have wide, plentiful distribution.
* You are assuming all readers adhere to a similar mindset.

Promotional Tools (Examples)

* Print advertising
* Digital advertising
* In-Store display, signage, and end caps

* Apps
* Television
* Radio
* Word of mouth

Differentiated Marketing

Practical Definition

The book will be marketed differently based on the differences of the audience (Example: You may position the book differently when selling to readers vs. librarians).

Pros

* Allows the author to highlight more than one feature or benefit of the book.

Cons

* Multiple marketing techniques among various groups can be costly.

* Inconsistent. With more than one marketing message, readers may find the themes of the book confusing.

Promotional Tools

* Advertising, listing, or mentions in: *Booklist*, *Library Journal*, *Kirkus*, *Romantic Times*, Ingram, Baker & Taylor, etc.

* Blog tours
* Conferences and events
* Social media
* Word of mouth

Concentrated Marketing

Practical Definition

All marketing efforts are focused on a select group of people.

Pros

* Focused—it allows you to market to one select group.

* An author of smaller name/brand recognition can compete with a larger one.

Cons

* Runs the risk of putting all of your eggs in one basket if the

targeted group rejects the book.

Promotional Tools

* Advertising, listing, or mentions in: *Booklist*, *Library Journal*, *Kirkus*, *Romantic Times*, Ingram, Baker & Taylor, etc.

* Blog tours

* Conferences and events which target specific groups: GENCON, *Romantic Times* Booklovers Convention, Malice Domestic, American Librarian Association, etc.

* Social media

* Word of mouth

* Digital advertising

Niche Marketing

Practical Definition

The book is designed and sold to one particular group. Anyone outside this group would not have an interest in the book.

Pros

* It allows the author to market to a set of people to solve a specific need.

* Highly focused.

* Affordable.

Cons

* Difficult to attract a larger audience other than the intended audience for the book.

Promotional Tools

* Google AdWords

* Speaking engagements

* Classes and lectures

* Endorsement from relevant sources or subject matter experts

* Direct mail

* Email campaign

* Newsletters

* Word of mouth

Now that the marketing strategies and their differences are defined, select one to help you find your target audience. To begin understanding target audience, start by building a profile of your ideal reader. This profile is your best guess of who your audience may be. Once you communicate to this group and get responses, you can evaluate the accuracy of your target profile by the audience you've attracted. To build a profile, include both demographic and psychographic information. The profile should include the target readers':

* Age
* Gender
* Location
* Marital status
* Ethnicity
* A list of similar authors they may enjoy
* Whether they shop in store or online
* Hobbies
* Interests
* Lifestyle

After building a completed profile, research where the targeted readers spend time. What social media sites do they use? Where do they purchase books? What websites do they visit? Do they prefer email or apps?

Once the target audience is profiled, the next step is for you to cultivate your fan base.

Begin by penetrating the social media space so you are online, visible, and attractive to your ideal readership. Advertise online and steer the tone and focus of the digital ads to the created profile. Blog where your ideal readers will see you.

Bestselling historical romance author Vicky Dreiling says, "The number one thing the author must do is create awareness. If readers don't know your book exists, they won't buy it."

Once you cultivate your readership, you should begin to engage with the target audience. Once comfortable with the audience, survey them against the assumptions made in the created profile. Adjust your promotional tools to match your survey results, and if there is a vast difference in your assumed target audience and your actual audience cultivated through promotions, readjust the targets to match the survey results and begin your outreach efforts again.

The end goal is to communicate your marketing message to the target audience. To build long-lasting rapport with the audience, you must work to make an emotional connection with your readership. Building a connection means building trust. To build trust and a relationship with readers, avoid using the "hard sell." The hard sell is an aggressive way of selling a product and is usually reserved for products that are hard *to* sell. The readership you cultivate must never feel "sold to." Therefore, it is to your advantage if you master the art of soft-selling.

According to *The Merriam-Webster Dictionary*, the definition of soft sell is the use of suggestion or gentle persuasion rather than aggressive pressure.

Soft-sell marketing is subtle, persuasive, and low pressure. The goal of soft-sell marketing is relationship building without aggressively pitching your book to readers. Once a relationship with your readership is created, selling will feel less forced, more natural and conversational. Soft-sell marketing is effective because you bond with your readership and create a lasting relationship over time.

As an example for this book, *New York Times* bestselling romance author Tawny Weber contributed three tweets written using hard-sell marketing. Then, she provided the same tweets written incorporating a soft-sell message. See the differences?

Hard Sell

1. How's Mission: Fake Engagement going to go? Find out in *A SEAL's Kiss* http://tawnyweber.com/as4 #SexySEALs

2. Hot, sexy and brooding . . . Check out Brody Lane in *A SEAL's Salvation*! #SexySEALs http://tawnyweber.com/as3

3 .#FREE *A SEAL's Surrender* by @TawnyWeber: http://:tawnyweber.com/as3 #free #HarlequinBlaze #kindle #nook #ibooks

Soft Sell

1. OMG, A fake engagement. *A SEAL's Kiss*. Would you ever fake an engagement?

2. Like hot, sexy and brooding heroes? I'd love to know what

you think of Brody Lane. http://tawnyweber.com/as3 *A SEAL's Salvation*

3. A free book? Yes, please. #FREE *A SEAL's Surrender* http://:tawnyweber.com/as2 #HarlequinBlaze #kindle #nook #ibooks

The second set of messages use a friendly tone. The tweets are conversational in nature, and the purchase of the book is implied without the use of hard-selling. A tip for writing soft-sell messages is to read the message aloud. If you feel the message says, "buy my book," re-write it.

Below are some additional tips for how you can become comfortable with soft-sell marketing.

* Believe in the book. Selling a book is difficult. When others see the emotional connection you have to your work, they will begin to care about the book as well. Clearly communicate to your readership why they should choose this book over another.

* Try relaxed networking. That is, connect without an agenda. Networking with the purpose of getting to know your audience relieves sales pressure.

* Build relationships. Seek additional ways to bond with your audience other than with books. Communicate your likes and passions.

* Open networking. Network outside your genre. Make contacts. Even though you may not write in the same genre as another author, chances are they know someone who writes what you do—or likes to read what you write.

* Offer freebies. Building bonds with your readership can sometimes mean giving away something. Share information, provide excerpts, or offer free books to your loyal readership. If you write nonfiction, it's important to educate first, sell second. For fiction writers, the occasional free read for your fans serves a dual purpose. First, it rewards your readership, and second, a free read can draw in readers who are not familiar with your work.

* Join forces. Find a fellow writer who you can partner with, and who will endorse you and share your book in social media.

* Repeat. Write your message three times, each time employing

the soft-sell technique. Use the third.

Key takeaways from this chapter:

* A target audience is a subset of the buying public who will deem your product or service worthy of purchase.

* A marketing strategy is needed in order to find a target audience.

* A positioning statement is a series of sentences which conveys your book's unique value to each buying group.

The four basic types of marketing strategies are: Mass Marketing, Differentiated Marketing, Concentrated Marketing, and Niche Marketing.

* Mass marketing works best when nothing more is needed to sell the book than the author's name and the book itself.

* Differentiated marketing is a concept where the same product is marketed differently based on the needs of different audiences. The crux of a differentiated marketing plan is that you can "argue" the multiple benefits of your book to find your target audience.

* Concentrated marketing is where all of the marketing efforts are focused on a select group of people.

* Niche marketing is a form of marketing where the product is solely designed to fit the needs of one specific group.

* Building a profile of your target audience should include both demographic and psychographic information. The profile should include the target readers' age, gender, location, marital status, ethnicity, hobbies, interests, lifestyle, buying patterns, and a list of like authors they enjoy.

* You can use surveys to evaluate the assumptions you made when creating your target audience profile.

* The end goal is to communicate your marketing message to your target audience.

Chapter Three

Brand and Platform. What's at Stake?

Brand is the process of attaching an idea to a product. A product's brand works to persuade the public to believe the idea by consuming the product. Above all else, brand is perception. For an author, brand means the author's identity. Collectively, it is how the author wants people to think, feel, and talk about their work. It is how the author will be known and what he or she will be known for. Brand identifies the author in the mind of the reader and delivers on the promise it makes to the reader.

The idea of branding existed long before authors began creating brands for themselves. Brand pioneer Walter Landor (1935-1995), founder of Landor Associates, left his mark in the business world by helping to increase the recognition of some of the world's top companies, including Levi's, Kellogg's, and Bank of America. Landor is quoted as saying, "Products are made in the factory, but brands are created in the mind."

Yet, an author has an advantage over industry. Brand must appeal to the emotions of the consumer, and an author's most powerful tool to support their brand is the emotions they evoke from their readership.

Some authors choose not to have a brand and simply rely on the work to speak for them, while others may not understand why having a brand benefits themselves or the reader. For marketing purposes, every author should have a brand. But, why? What's the point?

The answer is simple: to stand out in a crowd. Agatha, Anthony, Macavity, and Mary Higgins Clark award-winning, bestselling author and 2013 President of Sisters in Crime ®, Hank Phillippi Ryan sums up the importance of having an author brand:

"Creating a brand is a no-brainer. We grew up with brands . . . and use them every day. It is a way to let the buyer know what they are getting.

"Think of how we discuss items that don't have a brand . . . An off-brand, a generic. That can be the kiss of death for a product, right? We always think about whether we should buy that.

"When you walk into a bookstore, you look for the labels on the shelves, to know what you're getting. If you want a mystery or romance, you go to the parts of the store that are branded that way.

"A new author might brand herself by comparison. I often say if you like Lisa Scottoline, or Linda Fairstein, you'll like my books. I can do that because those authors are so 'well branded' that it's shorthand for what will be inside. The accomplished, professional, and successful bestselling Linda Fairstein would never show up at the Edgars in a miniskirt and platform heels, correct? That would be off-brand. I present myself as a bestselling author and experienced Emmy-winning investigative journalist. Would I dress in ratty jeans and a sweatshirt? (Yes, indeed . . . but only at home!) The public image needs to be protected, though—very important!— it can only work if it's genuine.

"So for me, everything I do, I run through my mental brand filter. It's important to emphasize here: This is not always conscious. And doesn't have to be. Because the branding is the genuine me. I know how I want to look, I know how I want my bookmarks to look, I know how I want my ads to look, I know the image I want them to portray. . . . Luckily, that image is the real me. With good lighting, of course.

"And I want people to have the feel of 'Hank'. I want them to say, 'Oh, that looks like a Hank book.' With, crossing fingers, the added response of . . . "And that means I will like it!" People want to know what they're getting; they don't want to have to guess. Having a good brand means you're reliable, dependable, desirable. It means if they liked what they got the last time, they're going to get it again. That's good. Having a scattershot image means you never know, it's a risk, I'm not sure. I hope readers will not only be drawn to my books, but to the person who wrote them."

To add to Ms. Ryan's point, the most critical part of brand-building is authenticity. Do not build a brand using short-term trends and fads. A brand should be designed to endure and not appear dated five to ten years in the future.

After the brand is created, how will you know it is correct? How will you know it resonates with readers? Brand should be deeply rooted in authenticity because it is evaluated:

* By what you accomplish. Do you deliver the brand promise through the work? For example, if the brand statement promises thrills and chills, does the book deliver?

* By your conduct. Are you knowledgeable about the topic or themes in the book? Did you do the necessary research?

* By what you say. Do you truly believe in the work?

* By what others say about you. What do reviewers and readers say about the book?

Knowing that your brand will be evaluated and judged helps to keep your brand on track. Think of your brand statement as putting a stake in the ground that says, "This is what I'm all about." For your brand not to waver, it's important to:

* Define it. Write it down. If you want to "try it out" before going public with it, write it down and post it near your workstation. Check that your brand agrees with what you are writing.

* Create demand. Keep readers hungry by writing the best book possible.

* Keep the brand promise with supporting actions. You should deliver the promise you make to the reader. However, this promise does not have to be only reader-focused. You may also want to keep promises made by your brand through public speaking—if you are an expert on a particular topic—or through educating other writers.

* Implement brand in everything you do. Again, from Ms. Ryan's earlier comments, she lives her brand by dressing and carrying herself in a way that supports her brand.

* Live the brand every day. Your brand should be rooted in authenticity.

Cultivating a brand sounds intimidating. It's not, if the brand is developed as a part of who you truly are and it's rooted in authenticity. For you to begin developing a personal brand, you are encouraged to perform a self-interview. Write down the answers to the following questions:

* What is it about your work that speaks to your passions?

* What makes you unique?

* How would you describe your voice?

* Look at your body of work. What are the common themes?

* Write two or three power words associated with your book. (Examples of power words are: Thrilling, Sexy, Steamy, Murder, Forbidden, Daring, Confessions, Stunning, No-risk, etc.)

* Answer the question: what is your book's emotional appeal?

Next, examine the answers to the above questions. Circle the power words. Then, using the selected power words, compose a statement, in less than ten words, that describes both you and the work using answers from the above questions.

The statement should clearly communicate who you are. It should be simple and memorable. The statement should inspire both you and the reader.

A brand statement provides the reader a preview of what you and your books are about. A brand statement should be neatly stated in less than ten words. Brand statements can be used for writing fiction and nonfiction. Below is a list of romance authors and their brands:

* Sara Humphreys: Paranormal Romance of a Different Breed (novelromance.net)

* Robin Covington: Sizzling Romance. Burning Up the Sheets One Page at a Time. (robincovingtonromance.com)

* Emma Leigh Reed: Where Broken Trust Is Healed by the Power of Love (emmaleighreed.com)

* Laura Moore: Rugged Heroes. Strong Heroines. Unbridled Passion. (lauramoorebooks.com)

However, a brand statement isn't solely used by romance authors. Below is an example of how a brand applies to a blogger:

* Sarah Wendell: All of the Romance, None of the Bullshit (smartbitchestrashybooks.com)

Here, brand is used for nonfiction:

> * Jennifer Fusco: Practical Marketing Advice for Writers (<u>marketordie.net</u>)

The above brand statements are crafted to give the reader a glimpse into the author and a brief description of what the reader may find. The statements allude to the author's genre, theme, whether the work is fiction or nonfiction, and (if the author is writing romance) heat level. Effective brand statements let the reader know what to expect before they begin reading.

Once a reader has engaged with an author's brand, tried their product, and returns for a repeat purchase, brand loyalty is built. However, a more intriguing question is why do readers return to purchase books by the same author over and over? Because brand brings the reader and author together. Brand has the ability to:

> * Enhance the reader's self-esteem, especially in the case of nonfiction.
> * Identify the reader with a peer group.
> * Speak to the reader's passion.

Paranormal romance author Sara Humphreys has a loyal, growing, and interactive readership. She says, "It's been my experience that romance readers really enjoy getting to know the author personally. By keeping your brand consistent and familiar, it reassures the readers that they know who you are as an individual. Then, when they read your books, it's like visiting with an old friend." Brand can make the reader feel that they are part of an exclusive club, rewarded by your work and attention.

However, developing a brand is not for published authors alone. Aspiring authors need to think about brand prior to publication. Why? Because brand is part of your overall platform. For aspiring authors, the brand may not need to be fully communicated to readers, as it should be with published authors; however, agents, editors, and publishers will need assurances that you know marketing is as much your responsibility as it is the publisher's.

Literary agent Nicole Resciniti of The Seymour Agency agrees. She says, "In today's publishing climate, it takes a collective strategy implemented by the publisher and author to generate success. Authors control their own destiny to a large degree in regard to how hands-on they want to be in their marketing approach. Can an author write a great book, make it available to readers, and simply wait to be discovered? Well, sure. But the likelihood of success diminishes. For the author who builds her platform, extends herself with social media, and targets her readers specifically, we see much higher sales. Those are the types of authors we want to work with."

Gwen Hayes, Former Senior Editor for Entangled Publishing, echoes Ms. Resciniti's sentiment, and, in an interview for this book said, "Ideally, before signing a debut author, I like to check that there is some sort of branding in place. If nothing else, to show that the author understands the importance of social media in the scheme of things. And to show that the author hasn't chosen a pen name that belongs to a serial killer or porn star. Also, there is nothing worse than looking up an author's Twitter handle and finding that she is all-negative-all-the-time. I wanted to work with professionals who know how to have fun while remaining . . . well, professional."

By having a preliminary brand in place, this shows the prospective agent, editor, or publisher that the author has a grasp of brand-building.

Aspiring authors may include their brand statement as part of their:

* Email signature
* Blog
* Website
* Business cards

While marketing is never more important than writing, the time period before you are published provides a great opportunity for you to learn the business end of writing as you seek publication. The aspiring author should be aware that, at some point, marketing will become part of their job.

Brand and Brand Endorsements

Sometimes, endorsements by other authors are used to enhance a brand. These endorsements usually appear on the front or inside cover of the work. When an author endorses a fellow author, it creates brand association in the mind of the reader. While an endorsement may not essentially be written as *if you like X, you will also like Y*, subliminally, that is the message the reader receives.

Endorsements are powerful. They help you stand out. Being endorsed by a fellow author in a genre can bestow great attention on you. *New York Times* bestselling author Loretta Chase was interviewed for this book regarding the endorsement of her work by Julia Quinn.

Q.) On your covers, Julia Quinn calls you, "One of the finest romance authors of all time." How does that make you feel?

Ms. Chase: "Pretty fine. When I first saw it, my jaw dropped. I emailed her right away and thanked her. I was restarting at my former publisher after an interval elsewhere, and they wanted something on the cover from one of the genre's superstars. She was very generous to give me such a knockout endorsement."

Q.) Do you believe there is power in the author endorsements?

Ms. Chase: "I believe publishers wouldn't seek them if they hadn't economic proof of their power, because they can be a large hassle to round up. Yet I do wonder about the value. Because one sees so many, on every book, and often the same authors are endorsing so many books—it can seem meaningless. And sometimes I'm buying a book in spite of an endorsement by an author whose work is not on my favorites list. OTOH (on the other hand), I was debating about buying a detective story when I read Stephen King's endorsement. I've read only a few of King's books because, while I *love* his voice and have tremendous respect for him, horror is not my cup of tea. The thing is, I wasn't used to seeing his name on detective novels, and his one sentence endorsement was smart and funny and apt. (I was so jealous. If I could write endorsements like that, I might actually consider writing endorsements.) I decided to try the book—and loved it! So there's my clue why publishers and authors suffer so much to get them."

Sometimes your editor will assist in seeking out endorsements by providing an advance copy of the work for the endorsing author to read. However, sometimes you may want to reach out on your own to request an endorsement (sometimes called a blurb) for the book.

If you desire to seek out an endorsement on your own, it is important to follow endorsement etiquette. Below are tips for properly seeking out an endorsement:

* Solicit endorsements from authors in the same genre.

* Read widely within your genre. It is important to become

familiar with who you are seeking an endorsement from and how they write, because an endorsement builds an association.

* Network. You are more likely to solicit an endorsement from someone you know.

* Send the author a well-crafted query. Tell them why you believe they are the best person to endorse the work. Seeking an endorsement from an author you do not know may best be arranged by the editor. If you are soliciting an endorsement from a fellow author who you do not know, familiarize yourself with their work. Let the author know of your admiration and tell them why they may enjoy your book. Ask for the endorsement, and then politely ask if they would like to read an advance copy.

* Be prepared to accept no as an answer. Do not take the rejection as a personal slight. Authors may have deadlines or commitments that prohibit the available time needed to give a proper endorsement.

* If the author declines, accept no, and do not press further.

If the author agrees:

* Communicate the schedule and make them aware of any deadlines.

* If you are looking for a specific theme, let them know what you are looking for.

* Ask how they wish to see their name on the endorsement.

* Once you have a finished copy, send it to them with a note of thanks.

It is perfectly acceptable for a book cover not to contain an endorsement. Just as they can be powerful, risks can also be associated with endorsements. Potential risks are:

* Image changes. If an author endorses you in one genre, then the endorser becomes better known in a different genre, this may lead to reader confusion.

* Overexposure. If the author endorses everyone in the same genre, it may lead to a "watered-down" effect.

* Overshadowed brand. If the endorser is "too famous," the endorsement may take the attention away from the author.

The interview with Loretta Chase showed the opinions of the author on the receiving end of an endorsement, but what does being asked to endorse a book mean to the author who is providing the endorsement? *New York Times* bestselling contemporary romance author Kristan Higgins is often asked to "blurb" fellow authors. Ms. Higgins was interviewed for this book. She provided the answers to the following:

Q: Do you have a limit on the number of books you endorse?

Ms. Higgins: "I don't have a hard and fast number, but I try not to overdo it. In the past year or so, I've been asked to endorse two or three books a week, and obviously, I can't say yes to all of those. I only blurb books in my genre (almost without exception). Right now, I blurb maybe one or two books a year."

Q. How are you approached for an endorsement? By the author or the editor, or both?

Ms. Higgins: "Both. I also get requests through my agent and publicists."

Q. Do you believe that "over-endorsing" waters down your brand?

Ms. Higgins: "I don't know about my writing brand, because that's not something I spend a whole lot of time thinking about . . . to me, brand is like personality, and it's evident in just about everything I do. But I do think too many endorsements can water down my credibility with readers. It's like having a lot of friends; sure, I have a lot of friends, but just like everyone, I also have an inner circle. The books I blurb are my inner circle books, if that makes sense. It doesn't mean I don't like and thoroughly enjoy other books out there, but the ones I blurb are the books I find really special."

Q. When you are blurbing a book, what do you believe the reader wants to know?

Ms. Higgins: "More than anything, I think a good blurb tells the reader how the book made me feel . . . and therefore, hopefully, how it will make them feel. Because that's what reading is all about—experiencing the emotion of the story."

An author endorsement is a channel of brand communication. Having an author act as your brand's spokesperson gives you credibility in the marketplace, and sometimes, helps to bolster the attention you deserve.

Key takeaways from this chapter:

* A practical definition of brand is the process of attaching an idea to a product in the mind of the public. Brand should be synonymous with the outcome of the product.

* You need a brand to help you stand out in a crowd.

* The most critical part of brand building is authenticity. Do not build a brand on short-term trends and fads.

* Design a brand to last over time.

* Brand statements provide the reader a preview of what you and your books are about in a truncated message.

* Aspiring authors should think about their brand prior to publication.

* Endorsements from fellow authors are used to enhance a brand.

* An author endorsement is a channel of brand communication. In essence it is to say, if the reader likes this brand, he or she will probably like that brand, too.

Chapter Four

Many Names, Many Brands

"Most people know that Mark Twain was the alias of Samuel Langhorne Clemens. The outing of Richard Bachman as a pen name used by Stephen King was well-publicized and inspired King's novel, *The Dark Half.* And, Joanne Rowling's publishers weren't sure that the intended readers of the Harry Potter books—pre-adolescent boys—would read stories about wizards written by a woman, so they asked her to use her initials on the book instead of her full name. Rowling didn't have a middle name, though, and had to borrow one from her grandmother Kathleen to get her pen name J.K. Rowling." (Matt Soniak, "*How 8 Famous Writers Chose Their Pen Names,*" Mentalfloss.com, June 14, 2013. Web, May 26, 2014)

This chapter is focused on pen names and brand-building. In today's digital world, it is false to assume you can hide your identity simply by crafting a pen name. And, it is equally false to assume you aren't required to build a brand when using a pen name. For each pen name you create, you must also create a supporting brand.

A pen name can be any name you select, as long as it is not already taken.

If you do not want to publish under your real name, deciding on a pen name can be difficult. Listed below are tips for creating a pen name:

　* Use an element of your real name. For example, if your birth name is Kimberly Joanne Smith, maybe you want to publish under Kim Smith or K.J. Smith.

* Consider the genre. Using the example above, if you were creating a pen name for mystery or thrillers, K.J. Smith may appeal to the readership, whereas Kimberly Smith may appeal more to a romance audience.

* Make it memorable. Creating an overly complex or too generic name can work against you. Try using a unique spelling to make your pen name stand out. Continuing with the example, the author may want to spell her name Kym Smith.

* Search the name. Once you have found a satisfactory name, search the Internet to ensure the name is not already in use. Use care to avoid celebrity names, or names of famous fictional characters.

* Play. If you want to capitalize on a specific ethnicity or heritage, try using behindthename.com. This site is a free, interactive website which contains a name-generating database. From the home page, this site can also be used to research the meaning and origin of names.

* Say it out loud. Practice an introduction using the pen name. Does it roll off the tongue? Evaluate the name based on how natural it sounds. Solicit opinions from friends or fellow writers.

Before publishing under a pen name, it is important to understand the pros and cons of a pen name. There are many advantages for using a pen name, such as:

* Artistic freedom. Writing under a pen name can lend itself to a certain amount of artistic freedom, especially for an author who already has an established brand.

* Fresh start. Sometimes, books do not sell as much as the publisher would like. Or, the book was not widely received by its intended readership. This can lead an author to start over with a pen name to recover from a dismal sales history.

* Avoid audience confusion. While cover art and the book blurb help to identify the proper audience for a book, if you write both for the adult and young adult market, it is wise to consider a pen name, especially if the books created for the adult market have explicit violence, horror, sexuality, or adult themes.

* Professional distance. Not all authors have the luxury of writing full-time; therefore, to maintain professional distance, you may create a pen name to separate you from your day job.

While there are "pros" to using a pen name, there are also "cons" to be considered. The potential downside of using a pen name can be:

* No association. If you build a readership under one brand, it is misleading to believe that that same readership will follow you into a new brand. While some of the readership may cross over, the new brand may not appeal to all. Also, it may be difficult for you to bridge the gap in the mind of the reader that you are published under more than one name.

* Difficult to break away. Being well-known can be a blessing and a curse for an author. While authors love reader engagement and loyalty, it can also create a sense of "type-casting" for an author in which he or she may find it difficult to break away from a success in order to try something new.

* Creates reader confusion. A pen name within the same genre can lend itself to reader confusion. To combat reader confusion, make sure the differences between the books written under the pen names are clear.

Contemporary romance author Cynthia D'Alba writes using a pen name. She began building her brand using her pen name prior to publication. Ms. D'Alba provided rationale on why she chooses to write under a pen name:

"I elected to use a pen name when I started writing. My reasons were multifold. My legal name is rather common (as evidenced by the number of bill collectors who call looking for other people with my name) and bland. Additionally, there is already a book published by someone using my legal name. Plus, I live in a relatively small community. If I wrote under my legal name, I would be too easy to find. Frankly, a number of people who live here know my legal and pen names and I don't worry about that. However, the reality is that writers collect stalkers for a variety of reasons, and my husband and I felt it would be safer to use a pen name.

"Another reason I elected to go with a pen name is marketability. I wanted a name that would be unique and memorable, and, as I noted, my legal name doesn't fulfill that requirement. I wanted a name that readers would remember, even if they hadn't read my books. But I wanted a name that wasn't so strange as to have readers scratching their heads wondering what planet was actually my home.

"When I decided to use a *nom de plume*, one of the considerations was where I would be shelved in a bookstore. Today, that aspect isn't as important to me as I focus primarily on digital books, but when I started writing, print was my target. I wanted my books to be shelved high or at least at eye level, not on the bottom shelf. I also wanted to be near a popular writer, hoping that her/his readers would find me while seeking the more established writer. But I also took into account book signings, where I would be located, who would be seated near me, etc. I wanted to be near the beginning of the authors for a signing, hoping to catch readers as they entered the signing, and not at the end, where readers might not find me. My writer name is a combination of a family name with the name of my husband's favorite actress! (True story.)

"One of the early lessons I learned from fellow writer Kay Thomas was to use my pen name solely as my identification in the writing world. In other words, not to use 'real name writing as pen name' on my emails, business cards or any other promotional materials. Which name is a reader supposed to remember? It's my pen name. I want that name in a reader's head, so why confuse the issue with two names? So, in the writing world, my pen name is branded on every promotional item I have. Even when I served on the RWA Board of Directors, I used my pen name on everything (as did the other board members). I recently pulled my name from a newspaper article because the editor insisted on using my legal name instead of my pen name. Since the article was about romance writers, I felt my legal name had nothing to do with the story and would only confuse people. I feel strongly on this point . . . my *nom de plume* for writing is the only name I need to be identified with within the writing world."

No matter if you choose to publish using a single pen name or multiple pen names, you must communicate the brand created to support each. If you are published under more than one name, it is important that the differences among the brands be distinct and easily understood.

Urban fantasy author Kate Locke also writes young adult fiction under the name Kady Cross, historical romance under Kathryn Smith, and steampunk romances under the name Kate Cross. She says, "The decision to use other names came about quite by accident. I had decided on

Kady Cross for my YA books, but my adult editor asked if I could use a different name for my steampunk romances. I chose Kate Cross because it was so close to Kady. Then, I chose another name for my urban fantasy novels because they were so very different from my romances. I just sort of 'fell' into having all these names." Kate's website, <u>alterkate.com</u>, is a fantastic example of how one author can support many different brands.

Communicating the variances among the names/brands may mean:

> * Setting up separate websites for each name. This will help to avoid confusing the reader. It is appropriate to link the sites to build the association between one name and another. Or, as in Kate's example, one website that distinctly describes each brand, and clearly communicates the differences.

> * Setting up separate profiles in social media. This may mean having more than one account on Twitter, Facebook, Pinterest, etc.

> * Visually communicating the differences in brands by using separate color schemes for each one. Choose a color to represent the tone of the brand and theme of the books. Implement the color scheme on websites, business cards, and promotional materials like bookmarks.

> * Understanding you are creating two separate fan bases. Yes, there may be crossover, but the crossover audience is not guaranteed.

Maintaining more than one identity is difficult, and sometimes, pen names lose their luster after a while. For this book, contemporary romance author Jessica Andersen discusses her creation of her alter ego, Jesse Hayworth:

"A few years ago, when the romance market shifted to some degree away from paranormals, and (more importantly) positive life changes made me less inclined to blow sh*t up in my books and more interested in writing funnier contemporary romances, there wasn't any debate: I was going to take a new name.

"Although it wasn't really that long ago in actual years, the industry landscape was very different. This was back when traditional publishers still worried about brick-and-mortar presales, which depended largely on the sales of your previous book. Since the sales of Jessica Andersen's latest were on the 'meh' side of life, she took a hiatus and Jesse Hayworth was born.

"I stuck with 'Jess' because I'm lucky if I remember to answer to my own name, never mind a pseudonym, and Hayworth is a combination of my unpronounceable married name and my maternal grandfather's last name. I initially wanted 'Haywood,' but that website was taken, and Jesse Hayworth's wasn't. So it was part sentiment, part practicality, and part me liking that my name had 'hay' in it when I was setting out to write modern-day cowboy books.

"At the time, the logic of taking a pseudonym seemed sound—in fact, it was pretty much treated as a given by my agent, my editor, and myself. In addition to the presale issue, my Jessica Andersen books were dark and complex, which was the complete antithesis of my sweeter, simpler, and more emotional dude ranch romances. The thought was that readers who had tried my darker series and found it not to their taste might avoid that name, so it was better to start with a clean slate.

"In retrospect, though, I wish I had stuck to a single name.

"Taking a pseudonym meant starting from scratch with a new website, new social media presence, new everything. I started about six months ahead of the first book's release, getting the website up and running, doing a weekly blog, making guest appearances, doing online ads . . . anything I could think of to change the answer to 'Have you read Jesse Hayworth's new excerpt?' from 'Who?' to 'I sure have. It rocked!' (at best) or at least something better than a puzzled look.

"It worked pretty well, all things considered, and the Jesse Hayworth books have found a solid readership. But all that marketing doubled up on efforts I was already making for the Jessica Andersen name, and I found that I lacked enthusiasm for maintaining two separate personas on Facebook. (My original idea was that Jessica could keep my usual crude sense of humor, while Jesse should be more refined. I totally couldn't pull that off and still be interesting.) So pretty soon, I started merging the two identities, first by diverting Jesse Hayworth fans to my established Facebook page, and then by combining the websites so both addresses go to a single portal page. And what do you know? Even my traditional print editor recently suggested that maybe we should add 'Jessica Andersen writing as Jesse Hayworth' to my e-books.

"So what changed? Well, the industry for one. With brick-and-mortar presales becoming less relevant (at least for mid-listers like me), it stopped being so important to get away from 'meh' numbers on prior books. Moreover, I think our (at least my) perception of the reader has changed with the digital revolution, and that we're taking a step back from doing things just because 'that's the way it's done.' I mean, I'm a reader, and I'm perfectly capable of pulling up an author's backlist and deciphering from the cover and blurb whether it's a genre I want to read. So why wouldn't I credit my fans with the same smarts? I will! I do! And if I had it to do all over again, I would stick with a single name."

Jessica Andersen did everything correctly with the creation of the Jesse Hayworth brand. But, as the market changed, she changed, too, and found a happy medium in merging the two separate brands. Did she waste her time performing the marketing work needed to bring Jesse Hayworth to life? No. Absolutely not. She broadened her readership and her career is now in a place where she can blend her audience and grow an even wider readership.

Ms. Andersen's technique of establishing, then merging, a brand is fairly common. For example, Nora Roberts also writes as J.D. Robb, and it is very common to see advertising communicating the differences in the two brands, and both are pen names. Both are very well-established, merged brands which allow Roberts to blend her readership for her romance and her futuristic suspense books. The key to a successful blending of brands among pen names is to ensure both brands are successful on their own merit.

Below are points you may want to evaluate before making the decision to merge brands:

* How long has the brand existed? If less than six months, it's possible the readership has not yet become fully engaged with a brand.

* Identify the synergies between the two brands. Answer the question, what will readers of both books like?

* Plan out communication. As in Jessica Andersen's example, her future plans are to include "Jessica Andersen writing as Jesse Hayworth" on her books, to further fuse the brands together.

* Communicate. Communicate. Communicate. Let the readership know of your many personas. Advertising and social media can assist well with this type of communication.

* Manage the migration over time, and keep in mind, some of the readers may never fully understand the differences in the brands no matter how much communication you do.

In summary, if you decide to use one or more pen names, you must build a brand to support each pen name. It is your choice to keep both names separate, or as Ms. Andersen has done, merge the two brands. It is important to constantly communicate the differences in your brand to avoid reader confusion. And, also, you must accept that no matter how much effort you put into those messages, a subset of the readership may never fully cross over because of the differences between the two brands. The use of pen names can be quite beneficial as long as you maintain the energy and enthusiasm needed for their support.

Key takeaways from this chapter:

* For each pen name you create, you must also create a brand to support it.

* It is important to understand the pros and cons of pen names prior to employing the use of one.

* There may be audience crossover from one pen name to another, but the crossover is not guaranteed.

Chapter Five

Brand Crisis and Managing Your Online Reputation

Blowbacks, flame-outs, meltdowns. At some point in your career, you may find your brand in crisis. A brand crisis is when you find that you are in the middle of a public relations nightmare. Rumors, blogs, and online chatter can contribute to making an otherwise awkward situation worse.

Authors can't anticipate the cause. Flame-outs have occurred over everything from readers who voice their disappointment in a long-awaited release, to a misprint in the media, to the authors themselves having some kind of social media meltdown.

No matter the cause, you are not powerless in navigating nasty PR waters. In fact, if you add a few basic tools into your wheelhouse, like using Internet alerts and learning how to "spin a situation," you can prepare yourself to weather any storm.

Internet alerts such as Google Alerts (google.com/alerts) can be a beneficial tool in notifying you of online mentions. By filling out an online form, you will be notified regarding any online activity which will allow you to monitor your name, book title, or any other keyword on which you wish to receive updates. At the time of this book's publication, Google Alerts does not monitor social media activity, like Facebook and Twitter. The benefit of Internet alerts is that the alert does the work of monitoring your online presence for you.

New York Times bestselling romance author Tawny Weber says, "I found Google Alerts to be spotty and unreliable. There is a great free tool called Mention. en.mention.com that not only tracks Internet mentions, but Facebook and Twitter as well. For every one Google Alert I receive, I receive four hundred mentions. I love it."

No matter the platform, Internet alerts can assist if newspapers and blogs get information wrong. If you notice a misprint in an article, kindly advise the reporter of the misprint via email and ask for a correction, or in the worst cases, a retraction of the story. Plan to monitor the news outlet for several weeks, or, in some cases, months if the magnitude of the misprint is great. Obtain hardcopies of the article (and retraction or correction) where possible. If you prepared any notes for the reporter prior to an interview, keep the notes and ensure they are dated.

Evaluate if you can spin the misprint to your advantage. If you use an article which contains a misprint, call out the error upfront. The key to the "PR spin" is keeping ahead of any potential damaging situation. Also remember that if you promote the article, also promote the retraction or correction. This provides a one-two punch in the media as well as written proof that the misprint was the reporter's error, not yours.

Online crises, such as receiving multiple bad reviews, can be harder to manage simply because of the speed of communication. However, you can help to manage the unfortunate situation by staying calm and doing the right thing.

A few years ago, mystery author Kate George, creator of the Bree McGowan series, found herself in a crisis when a bad file of her story which contained multiple errors was uploaded and made available for sale. Readers noticed and voiced their unhappiness, which resulted in bad reviews that affected her sales. Through effective management, Kate rectified a potential harmful situation that might have damaged her overall brand if she'd chosen to ignore it. She details her account of what happened below.

"It was the beginning of the digital revolution, and I didn't realize that anything I did online would be there to haunt me forever. I figured if there was a mistake, someone would tell me, I'd fix it, and that would be the end of it.

"Hah!

"I don't really know where the bad file came from. My publisher was kind enough to send me the final of the book before it was formatted for print. I suppose it's possible that somehow they sent me the wrong file, but it's equally as possible that I uploaded the wrong file. I just don't know. What I do know is that I should have checked every single page myself before I hit publish—and I didn't.

"I personally asked people who read the e-published version of my book if they found any problems. I don't think one person told me they noticed anything wrong. I suppose those were the people that read for the story and ignored the formatting snafus and typos—oh yes, there were many typos along with the formatting problems.

"I think the book had been out over a year before I started getting bad reviews for the formatting. One reviewer said it was the worst formatted e-book she had ever read. So I did what I thought would solve the problem, I went through, page by page, reformatting and fixing typos. Then I noted on the Amazon page that it had been reformatted.

"That's when reviewers started leaving outraged comments saying it had *not* been reformatted. So I paid to have a professional reformat it. I put that up. I still got complaints about the formatting. That's when I discovered that just because you fix a book doesn't mean the readers will get the new copy. And apparently, at that time (I sure hope they've fixed it by now), Amazon had a number of different servers, and just because you uploaded a new copy to one server, that didn't necessarily mean that the other servers would have it.

"I was seriously frustrated. My sales were dropping, and I couldn't seem to do anything to remedy the problem. So I did the only thing I could—I spread the word that I would either replace or refund readers who were unhappy with the book. I contacted everyone who left a negative review and offered them the same deal. And that's when I discovered that many of the negative reviewers had gotten the book for free. That made me just the tiniest bit crazy, but I continued to offer readers their money back or a clean copy of the book. I think maybe two readers took me up on it.

"A number of one or two star reviews actually liked the story but rated it low because of the formatting errors; they didn't want a new copy either. Another thing I discovered is that people love to jump on the negative bandwagon. They'll trash your book for no other reason than they can, and all the offers of refunds will not make them happy. Just for the record, I never asked any of them to delete their reviews. I wasn't trying to buy them off in order to get the negative reviews expunged; I just wanted them to have a positive feeling when they heard my name.

"Hopefully, there are some people out there who appreciated getting a refund or fresh books; that was the point, after all, but my books were still not jumping off the e-shelves. Even pricing the books at ninety-nine cents or free didn't create the jump in downloads I'd experienced in the past—and this was with the professionally copyedited and formatted version.

"So I rebranded. New covers, new tag lines. I got the print rights back from my publisher and used CreateSpace to make paperback books with matching covers. That helped. Over time, the sales have crept back up. Releasing the third in the Bree MacGowan Series created a substantial increase in sales and I learned to ignore the problems I created because I didn't understand the nature of the web, Amazon, reviewers, and probably human nature, too.

"The negative reviews are still out there. They always will be, and there always will be more, but I choose not to focus my attention on the negative. I always respond to readers who contact me directly, and I thank them if they point out a mistake that I missed. Heck, I thank them even when I don't agree that what they are seeing is a mistake.

"I've also learned that trying to please everyone is just not possible, and I've stopped trying. When I write, I focus on who I know my readers to be. If I can make them happy, then I'm doing okay. And every time I finish a book, I give it to *two* copy editors—one, then another to catch as many typos as possible. I send it to a professional to format both for e-books and paperback books. Then, I double-check the proofs.

"Are they perfect? No. And truthfully, I'm not aiming for perfection. At some point, you have to let go of a book and send it out into the world. Because the best thing I can do to make my readers happy and leave them with a positive impression is to write them a new story. Because that's what my readers want—another glimpse into Bree MacGowan's world."

Ms. George masterfully handled what any author may see as their worst nightmare with grace and understanding. But that's not all. She realized she wasn't powerless to control the situation. Yes, she might not have been able to control the less than stellar reviews, but she learned valuable lessons from the situation and put a process in place to ensure it didn't occur a second time.

Learning something negative about yourself online that can affect your brand can come as a shock, and the first instinct may be to panic or react impulsively. Impulsiveness only makes the situation worse. So, before you lose your cool (or act like a nut), remember the acronym ACORN.

A—Acknowledge. If you discover a negative remark online which requires a response (and not all remarks do), communicate that you are saddened by the event and are working to repair the situation.

C—Communicate. When you find yourself in crisis, it is not the time to disappear. If you need help from other sources (editor, agent, publicist, or publisher) communicate this to the fan base, and in return, ask for their patience.

O—Offer assistance. If it is in your control, you may offer assistance in rectifying the situation. Maybe it's as simple as agreeing to pass along information or, as Ms. George said, she offered her readership a refund or a clean copy of the book.

R—Remain professional. Authors are emotionally invested in their work. They should be. Their books are an extension of themselves. However, it is not professional to take a negative review or comment as a personal attack. Even if you are attacked online, it is not in your best interest to retaliate.

N—Never engage. In other words, don't start the fight. You will always encounter the negative blogger, the bad review, the miserably unsatisfied reader. What's the popular cliché? Haters gonna hate. Well, in some cases, it's true. The important lesson is to know that, by engaging the negative blogger or bad reviewer, it may draw more attention than you would like. And, engaging unsatisfied readers will most likely not mitigate their misery. It may only fuel their fire to tell more people how not only the book made them unhappy, but so did you.

While reading this chapter, you may wonder how I know so much about PR nightmares and brand crises. The truth? In 2012, I faced my own brand crisis and below is my story.

"In addition to writing, I own a small business by the same name as this book, Market or Die. To build my brand, I thought I'd run some print advertising in the Romance Writers of America ® magazine, the *Romance Writers Report*. It was a very plain ad, which listed the services and prices for my marketing company. Little did I know that one ad would have me, my company, and my clients served up like fresh meat to a pack of starving wolves.

"It was fine for the folks on the online blog to question my company. There are companies who do take advantage of authors, but contrary to their belief, mine isn't one of them. However, on November 29, 2012, in sixty-one posts, I was accused of, among other things, being overpriced, knowing very little about marketing, and having a bit of a jargon problem (oh yeah, that one was my favorite).

"My first reaction: I hit the roof and said an over-abundance of swear words. But I did so in private. Once I calmed down and re-read the posts, I understood how the audience could be confused with the way some of the terms on my website were written. And, I resolved to change what they found issue with, but at the same time, chose to stand firm and defend myself and my business model against online bullies.

"I asked friends and clients to post on my behalf. It took me a day to get approval to post on the blog, and once I could, I responded professsionally and addressed their concerns. But voicing a response didn't help the matter. More posts appeared, hounding my clients about posting their sales after working with me and badgering them for concrete data on how my services were worthwhile. Obviously, my clients didn't post their sales numbers, nor give them anything they demanded as 'proof' I was legit, and eventually we made the decision to walk away and quit responding.

"I understood that no matter how I tried to defend my business, my knowledge of marketing, or my experience dealing with professionals in the romance writing industry, nothing I said was going to change their minds. It was impossible to rationalize with the 'Internet Brave.'

"So, I walked away.

"As long as my clients were happy, I was happy. That has been my working mantra from the day my company started, and is still true today. And, my clients must've been really happy because in 2013, Market or Die took second place in the P&E Poll for Best Promotional Firm, Site or Resource. Here's the link: critters.org/predpoll/final_tally_promotions.ht (I'm so proud!) And, feel a little vindicated, too."

In summary, when you find out about negative comments regarding your book or your brand, it hurts. You have the right to feel disappointed at learning of criticisms. However, in responding to negativity online, it's important to keep a professional distance between yourself and the comments, and not become overwhelmed by the emotion of the situation. You should help to rectify the circumstances if it is within your power, and most importantly, know when to walk away when it isn't.

Key takeaways from this chapter:

* A brand crisis is when you find yourself in the middle of a public relations nightmare.

* If a crisis arises over a misprint in the media, you can try to spin the misprint to your advantage.

* The key to a "PR spin" is keeping in front of any potential damaging situation.

* Before the author "acts like a nut", remember ACORN: Acknowledge. Communicate. Offer assistance. Remain professional. Never engage.

Chapter Six

Your Place in the Market—Keeping Readers for Life

Our marketplace thrives on cultivating relationships and personal selling. As more marketing work is falling to the authors, they are wearing the hats of not only content creator, but marketer and seller as well. This chapter focuses on an in-depth understanding of the AIDA Hierarchy of Effects marketing model, its evolution, and how, by understanding and adopting the model, you can keep attracting readers for life.

As mentioned in Chapter One, the four-layer model which is comprised of Awareness, Interest, Desire, and Action, is still relevant today. Lewis and Russell's theory was used as a basic principle and evaluation tool for advertising. However, today's marketing encompasses more than just traditional face-to-face selling and print advertising, and the AIDA model can be used for book marketing. Understanding the AIDA model, and what each phase stands for, is integral to promotional longevity and success. The basics of AIDA are:

A—Attention. (sometimes called awareness). Simply means attracting the attention of the buyer.

I—Interest. This phase raises awareness by focusing on the benefits of what is being sold.

D—Desire. This phase convinces buyers the product will satisfy their needs.

A—Action. The last phase directs the buyer toward the purchase.

The model is simple, effective, and proven over time. However, with changes in promotional tools like digital advertising, online reviews, and the use of social media, the AIDA model has evolved.

Professor Bambang Sukma Wijaya published a recent paper which said, "The development of Information Technology has radically changed the way people communicate and socialize; as well as a paradigm shift from product-oriented marketing to consumer-oriented marketing. Therefore the variables in the hierarchy of effects model needs to be updated in respond [sic] to the latest development in the notice of public power as a consumer audience." (*International Research Journal of Business Studies*, Vol 5. "The Development of Hierarchy of Effects Model in Advertising," 2012, 75-85)

According to today's modernized version of AIDA, it incorporates communication and satisfaction, taking into account the power of the consumer and their opinions.

Paraphrasing from his article, today's model looks more like this: AISDALSLove.

A—Attention. (sometimes called awareness). Attracting the attention of the buyer.

I—Interest. This phase raises awareness by focusing on the benefits of what is being sold.

S—Search. Today's informed consumer will perform the necessary searches for the products they want at the price they expect to pay. Searches can be internal, external, or both. An internal search involves what is recorded in the mind of the consumer, presumably based on past experiences.

D—Desire. This phase convinces buyers the product will satisfy their needs.

A—Action. Directs the buyer toward the purchase.

L—Like/Dislike. The result after the use of the product.

S—Share. With the advances of today's technologies, consumers can take action for or against a brand.

Love—Love/Hate. The buyer forms a permanent, cognitive feeling about the product.

But, what does AISDALSLove mean, and will understanding a formula created to measure effective advertising teach you how to identify readers who will assist in the promotion of you and your work? Yes.

How? Examine the diagram below. It explains how the AISDALSLove model can be used to attract a target audience.

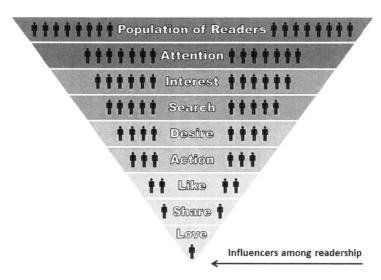

The top of the diagram depicts the mass population of general readers. The triangle represents the phase of the purchasing/engagement process for the general reader. Through these phases, the population of readers becomes smaller and more refined; this is how your fan base is formed.

For example, most readers pay attention to new books. They see books advertised online, they may see them in a store while browsing for other products, or they've enjoyed the author's previous books. Then, their interest is generated, most commonly from a striking cover image and compelling back cover copy. However, today's book consumers are smart, and spend wisely, so they perform the necessary research about the book and its author to get the best read for the best price. While searching, desire is formed; now the consumer is "on the hunt" for the work. This leads them to the action of making a purchase. Then they read. In the end, they like the book, and find it so pleasurable they must tell their friends. But, to this reader, sharing isn't enough because he or she loved the book. Love is where you will find your actual fans. In the love stage, these fans will go the extra mile for you, their favorite author. These are the people who will review your books, blog about your book, or send you fan letters. They may be few, but they are loyal. They are super fans.

Super fans will be your readers for life.

Cultivating a loyal readership sounds daunting, and you may believe you can do nothing other than write the best book possible and wait to be "discovered." Maybe, in a few cases, that course of action has worked. However, you will feel more powerful and less frustrated if you help yourself cultivate the necessary fan base needed to stay relevant in the marketplace.

You can assist in creating your fan base by assigning promotional tools and using them within each phase of the AISDALSLove process. An explanation of each is listed here.

Attention:

Think of the attention phase like a media blitz. The goal of this phase is to drive the reader to a place to learn more about your book. Advertising is a proven promotional tool in order to gain attention for a book. And, with the advances in digital advertising, it can be highly targeted to find the correct readership. Then, you can direct the reader to a website or link to a purchase site. Many online websites and social media platforms offer advertising. But, instead of advertising to the masses, your goal will be to target the reader you want. Before running any advertisement, I advise you to research the demographics for your genre to find your ideal book buyer.

For example, in 2010, Sisters in Crime released results of a study titled *The Mystery Book Consumer in the Digital Age*. In the first chapter of the document, the demographics of the mystery buyer were calculated. While this data has aged, the report revealed that in 2010:

* 68% of the mystery buyers are female.
* 48% of the buyers are over the age of fifty-five.
* 35% of mystery buyers live in the South.

Carl Kulo (R.R. Bowker, *"The Mystery Book Consumer in the Digital Age," Report*. [Bowker, 2010] sistersincrime.org. Web, June 5, 2014)

Using the demographic data, the mystery author would then be able to target the ad to women over the age of fifty-five who live in the South, and like to read mysteries. Through targeted social media advertising, the author has begun to slice off a piece of the general population of readers in order to find his or her ideal reader.

Demographics by genre can be found online, or by becoming a member of writers' organizations such as Sisters in Crime or Romance Writers of America, who make such data available to their membership. It is up to you to ferret it out and use it to cultivate a readership. And, it is this readership that will help you sustain momentum in the marketplace and carry you forward.

Interest:

Once you gain the buyer's attention, you must support the buyer through the interest phase by ensuring you are available and accessible. I encourage you to create a website, blog, or have a social media presence in order to keep the interest of the potential book buyer. According to the 2012 Romance Writers of America survey on "Activities of the Romance Buyer," 41% of romance buyers visited the author's website, 18% saw a promotional book trailer and bought the full book, 16% read an author's blog, while 13% followed the author on Facebook. The survey continues to report under "purchase influences":

Top "offline" factors in influencing purchase decisions:
* Enjoyed the author's previous books
* Book is part of a series they're reading
* Description on the back cover or flap
* Recommendation of a friend or relative

Top "online" factors in influencing purchase decisions:
* Online bookseller websites (Amazon.com, BN.com, etc.)
* Reading about it/seeing it online
* Seeing it on a bestseller list
* Author website

Top overall decision factors when deciding on a romance:
* The story
* The author
* It's part of a series
* Back cover copy

(Romance Writers of America, "Romance Reader Statistics" Survey.

rwa.org. [Bowker, Not dated] Web, June 5, 2014)

Therefore, to gain potential book buyers in the romance genre, romance authors would be wise to use the above list as a checklist and ensure their "bases are covered" and to capitalize on potential reader interest.

For example:

* If the book is part of a series, have you made the message clear to potential readers?

* Is the back cover copy compelling?

* Is the book hosted at all online retailers? Are links available for communication?

* Is your website both of professional quality and reliably hosted?

* Have you established a social media presence?

When a potential buyer is in the interest phase, it is important you do what you can to make all information about you and your work available and accessible.

Search

In marketing, using the term "search" makes our brain automatically think about the Internet. However, *search*, as described by Wijaya in the AISDALSLove process, means that the consumer will search for information about the product externally as well as internally.

Both producers and consumers are familiar with external searches, with the most common search engines on the Internet being Google, Bing, and Yahoo. And, when a consumer types questions or keywords, the search engine then uses a set of algorithms to produce a list of websites, returned in an order where the most popular, relevant information is listed at the top.

Search engine optimization helps to improve a website's ranking. Higher rankings among websites places the site at the top of the search results to assist consumers in finding what they are looking for. Words, titles, links between websites, and words inside links all help to improve a website's ranking, as well as the site's reputation and quality of content.

However, the internal search is where the author's brand can influence the reader. Wijaya says, "Internal search involves the consumer identifying alternatives from his or her memory. Consumers have stored in memory a variety of information, feelings, and past experience that can be recalled when making a decision. Consumers with a greater degree of knowledge and experience therefore have a greater ability to search internally. Specifically, researchers have examined the recall types of four types of information: (1) brands, (2) attributes, (3) evaluations, and (4) experiences (Alba, et al, 1991). Recall of brands refers to the set of brands that consumers recall from memory whenever problem recognition has been stimulated, recall of attributes refers to specific facts about a product or service, [and] recall of evaluations refers to our effort or attitudes (that is, our likes or dislikes), because our memory for specific details decays rapidly over time. Evaluations are more likely to be recalled by consumers who are actively evaluating the brand when they are exposed to relevant information. Meanwhile, recall of experiences refers to the internal search by recalling experiences from autobiographical memory in the form of specific images and the effect associated with them. (Bumgartner et al, 1992)"

By building a strong, consistent brand, constructed by your compelling storytelling and ability to evoke emotion from your readership, your brand can leave a lasting impression on memory for recollection by the internal search. Authors often say the greatest selling tool for a writer is their next book. This saying is validated by the consumer's internal search. One negative experience with a brand will be stored in the mind of the consumer, and the consumer will draw upon that experience when making a future purchase.

Desire

Your actions to support the desire phase are similar to those in the interest phase. Once the reader has searched (either internally or externally) for the book, you can support the desire phase by ensuring your book is available on every major outlet within your reach. You should ensure buy links are communicated on your blogs, websites, social media, advertising, newsletters, and book recommendation websites.

Action

To assist the reader in a purchase, you can ensure purchase links are shared and widely available during pre- and post-release. Below are fifteen suggestions of where to place purchase links:

   * Press releases. Ensure the purchase link is in the press release

and can be communicated in the media should they feature the book.

* Newsletters. Send the purchase link in the newsletter to all subscribers.

* Blog Carnivals. Blog Carnivals are online communities that are interested in and contain articles on various topics.

* Bloggers/Guest Blogging. Place the purchase links within the blog article.

* Advertising. Digital advertising should link to a purchase site.

* Social Media. Share purchase links on all social media platforms.

* Sponsorships. You may sponsor an event and communicate purchase information as part of your sponsorship.

* Apps. You may want to pay an app to feature your link, or create your own app for your books.

* Free Samples. Follow up any posted excerpt with a purchase link.

* Awards. If the work has won an award, communicate the purchase link along with the announcement.

* Book Trailer. Embed the purchase link in the video.

* Testimonials. Along with the endorsement or testimonial, include the purchase link where applicable.

* Conferences/Conventions. If you are planning to attend a conference, convention, or signing, place the purchase link for the book you will be signing on all communication.

* Featured Content via Info Graphics. Ensure the purchase link is on all visual communications.

* Contests. Most contests must contain a free entry option; however, contests are an avenue to communicate purchase availability.

Share

With both the speed and access to communication, opinions matter. Therefore, what is becoming more important to today's consumer isn't advertising or mass media, it is the opinions of their friends and others the consumer trusts. Wijaya writes, "The law of small numbers in the consumer's decision-making process whereby people expect information obtained from a small sample to be typical of the larger population (Tversky and Kahnman, 1971; Hoyer and Macinnis 2010) more strengthening [sic] the assumption of the role of the consumer experience-sharing in influencing other consumers. If friends say that a new hand phone by a particular group is really good or that the food at a particular restaurant is terrible, we believe that information, even if most people do not feel that way.

"In fact, reliance on small numbers is another reason that word-of-mouth communication can be so powerful. We tend to have confidence that the opinions of friends or relatives are more reflective of the majority than they may actually be.

"Moreover, growing users of digital social media today make the consumers become freer in expressing their experience to the world. Therefore, the key for brands is to empower consumers by delivering an exceptional experience that inspires them to share their stories."

The author's role is to understand the importance of sharing. Encourage the readership to share their enjoyment over a book and make recommendations. Historical romance author Vicky Dreiling spent many years in corporate marketing before beginning her career as an author. Below, Ms. Dreiling shares how she encourages fans and readers to share information about her books online.

"In the late nineties, when I was taking Consumer Behavior, a marketing class, my professor stressed the importance of including interactive items on websites. Yes, marketers were talking about engagement in 1999. If I may go back even further, my late father, who was in sales all of his life, knew the value of relationship marketing.

"The most important aspect of social media is engagement. As much as three-fourths of my engagement on Facebook is focused on the readers—not on me.

"I spent ten years in corporate marketing and conducted numerous focus groups. One day it occurred to me that I could learn a great deal from readers by asking them questions and probing for additional information, the same way I'd done with high-tech focus groups. Of course, this is not 'conducted' in a controlled environment, but nevertheless, I've learned a great deal about readers' preferences for covers, subgenres, e-readers, print books, historical time periods, favorite authors, heroine's ages in historical romance, etc. It's important to note that readers like to provide their likes and dislikes. As you may imagine, this is extremely valuable to me.

"I provide links on Twitter to let readers know about book giveaways, reviews, special promotional prices for my backlist books, and appearances. Occasionally, I hold short conversations with readers who want to let me know they enjoyed my book. One of my favorites came from a reader in Turkey.

"When I'm currently writing a book, I don't have as much time to engage with readers. However, I'll often share a few short lines from the book in progress on Facebook and occasionally on Twitter as well. The readers love to call me a tease, and it's all in good fun. I also show cover reveals and giveaways of my books on my Facebook author page.

"I hold a session on my Facebook timeline on Saturday mornings called Q&A Saturday. Recently, I asked the readers to share what they're reading. This is a really fun way for everyone, including me, to get reading recommendations from others. It's casual and fun for all of us.

"Beyond books, we also dish about TV shows and movies. *Downton Abbey* is quite popular with many readers. The speculation about the next episode is great fun for all.

"I belong to a writer's promotion group, and we help spread the word about each other's new releases via Facebook and Twitter.

"In addition, I have a preferred list of bloggers whom I've formed relationships with over the past three years. They're a great help getting the word out about my books and providing honest reviews.

"I use Pinterest to make collages of my books. This is particularly helpful for me as I'm a visual learner. It's an additional way to create awareness of my books.

"I think it's important for authors to have a good understanding of how any communication with readers works. A newsletter is an information source, but it is not a social vehicle."

Love

Love, or rather the love of a brand, can lend itself toward the impulse and repeat purchase. The love of a brand can entice the consumer to "try new things" based on the brand alone. The love between consumer and brand can strengthen or diminish over time based on the experiences. Wijaya says, "Supported by a good brand experience, this connection becomes stronger over time so that (it) creates brand loyalty and a sense of belonging to the advertised brand. There is no better way to build such a similarly long-lasting brand loyalty than continually nurturing brand relationship in order to ensure that brand and consumer remain connected."

Your goal in the last stage is to create a reward for reader (love) loyalty. You or your publicity team can create fan clubs (sometimes called street teams) to pull the readers in and give them a "behind the scenes" look into your world. You may also choose to reward readers by giving them exclusive sneak peeks, swag, or information in a specialized newsletter.

The readers who love an author want to connect. And, these are the relationships you must hold closest, because when author and story come together, it creates a positive brand experience for the reader, and one they are eager to repeat.

Throughout the process of engaging your readership, especially the readers who love your brand, it is important to remember four keys to building reader loyalty. They are:

* Craft dynamic teaser lines which promise a good payoff.

* Let the audience know they are buying something of value.

* Deliver the payoff.

* Reward loyalty.

Key takeaways from this chapter:

* AIDA stands for Attention, Interest, Desire, and Action.

* AISDALSLove modernizes AIDA and stands for Attention, Interest, Search, Desire, Action, Like, Search and Love.

* You can use the AISDALSLove methodology to discover your "super fans."

* You can assist in creating your own fan base using promotional tools within each phase of the AISDALSLove process.

* There are four keys to building reader loyalty: dynamic teaser lines which promise a good payoff, letting the audience know they are buying a product of value, delivering the promised payoff, and rewarding loyalty.

Chapter Seven

Building the Strategic Plan

This chapter covers the strategy you should learn in order to lay out a marketing plan. In this section, I will show you strategies for building an integrated marketing plan. You will learn strategy tools for decision making, such as SWOT analysis and Author Landscape Analysis. Once taught, both tools will be provided using real life examples.

Effective marketing plans are built upon two components: strategy and execution. *The Merriam-Webster Dictionary* defines strategy as the skill of making or carrying out plans to achieve a goal.

The benefits of spending time on your marketing strategy prior to jumping into book promotions will help you to:

* Learn where to spend your marketing budget.

* Learn what the target audience expects.

* Justify saying, "No, thank you," when unplanned opportunities present themselves, ones which may not fit into your plan.

The goal of this chapter is to teach three important marketing strategies: the positioning statement, the competitive author landscape analysis, and SWOT analysis.

Positioning Statements

The use of a positioning statement within a book marketing plan provides direction for your overall marketing. The positioning statement details what you expect to deliver to the reader and what result you expect from the delivery. In a positioning statement, you not only describe your target market, but also list how you expect to be perceived within that particular market.

If we were tasked with creating a traditional positioning statement for a product in the marketplace, we would ask, what is the consumer's problem and how does this product solve it? As an example, if we were asked to create a positioning statement for laundry detergent, and our company wanted to be known for offering the best detergent for the lowest price, we might focus on one or more perceived customer problems, such as getting the best stain-fighting power for a low cost per use. We would also need to list the advantages or attributes of the product the customers will want to know before buying our product. In the fictional laundry detergent example, attributes may be: the actual cost per use, newer scents, or an ingredient for stain removal.

Here, you are not being asked to solve a problem for readers. Book positioning statements should be created with more care than simple problem-solving. Instead, you should ask yourself what you hope to bring to the reader (either emotionally or educationally) through your book. And, by doing so, how do you believe you will be perceived?

Before you can craft a positioning statement, you must be able to:
* Name/Identify your target audience
* Name your brand
* Name your market
* State your position in the market
* List your attributes

Once you list the answers above, then you can simply fill in the positioning statement below.

Convince (*the target audience*) that (*the brand*) in the (*market*) can deliver (*state your position*) that (*because/why*) (*list relevant attributes and critical capabilities*).

Think of a positioning statement as a pitch. Except in a pitch, you would describe the book or series of books, but a marketing positioning statement speaks to your brand.

Example:

So that you can properly understand how to develop the statement, I've used *Market or Die* as an example.

> * Name/Identify the target audience: Fiction and nonfiction writers
>
> * Name the brand: *Market or Die*
>
> * Name the market: Educational "how-to" books for the writer's market
>
> * State the position in the market: Practical marketing advice
>
> * List the attributes: Writers must learn to market themselves in order to establish a presence in the marketplace, build relationships, and increase sales.

The positioning statement for *Market or Die* looks like this:

> Convince (*the target audience*) **writers of fiction and nonfiction** that (*the brand*) **Market or Die** in the (*market*) **educational "how-to" books for writers' market** can deliver (*state your position*) **practical marketing advice** (*because/why*) because (*list relevant attributes and critical capabilities*) **writers must learn to market themselves in order to establish a presence in the marketplace, build relationships, and increase sales.**

Example:

To create a positioning statement for fiction, rely on the emotional connection of author to reader, as contemporary romance author Laura Moore wrote for this example:

> Convince (*the target audience*) **contemporary romance readers** that (*the brand*) **Laura Moore** in the (*market*) **Romance Market** can deliver (*state your position*) **romantic sagas** (*because/why*) that (*list relevant attributes and critical capabilities*) **explore the love forged between two passionate individuals and the bonds that keep families strong.**

As you begin to create an outline of a marketing plan, you will place the constructed positioning statement in the beginning of the document. The statement will act as a checklist for the body of the plan, and ensure that all promotional efforts support the marketing direction for the brand. It may seem difficult to boil down your positioning, but working through the exercise can be invaluable. If you are unable to clearly communicate who you are and what you write, how is a reader supposed to?

SWOT Analysis

SWOT analysis was derived from a research methodology conducted at the Stanford Research Institute from 1960 to 1970 and is still in use today by businesses, researchers, and the like. For the author, SWOT analysis is a simple tool to use in understanding your strengths, weaknesses, opportunities, and threats. It can be used for strategic planning, brainstorming, or decision-making. It must also be described in detail to explain its usefulness in book marketing.

Below is an example of a SWOT analysis for a public library and an examination of its purpose within a community. To begin the analysis for the library, list all of the strengths of a community library. For example, a library's strengths might be:

* It is a quiet place to read, research, and relax.
* It is a free opportunity to read and use the Internet.
* It offers friendly, helpful librarians.
* It is open to everyone.
* It allows long "check-out" periods for books, returning in about four weeks

Continue to build a list of strengths for the library until the list is exhausted. Once the list is complete, begin listing the weakness for the library; these may be:

* Its hours. Information is not readily available twenty-four hours a day.
* It could offer outdated materials.
* There are late fees for books returned past the due date.

Continue to build a list of weaknesses for the library until the list is exhausted. For opportunities, list the opportunities the library could offer in the future to improve their marketability. This is how the library could provide value.

* Offer literacy programs.
* Offer weekly children's programs.
* Offer occasional author readings/signing opportunities.

* Offer a wide array of educational programs.

* Become a centralized place for community events.

Continue to build a list of opportunities until the list is exhausted. Then list the threats a library can face. It is important to list all of the potential threats to the function of the library. Be sure to list the competition and all potential negative impacts.

* The Internet is readily accessible elsewhere.

* Bookstores—brick and mortar, and online—offer the same books.

* Limited state or national funding.

Once the SWOT analysis is completed:

* Communicate the strengths to the target audience.

* Make a plan to take advantage of opportunities and combat the weaknesses using the identified strengths.

* Understand the threats.

In the library example, the goal would be to promote new opportunities within the library using its strengths, such as marketing it as a perfect place to hold events, like author readings and signings because it's free and open to everyone. Combat the threats. For example, to communicate the value of the library within a community, the marketer would promote the friendliness and helpfulness of the librarians who can provide timely assistance against long, time-consuming Internet searches. Address the weaknesses, where possible, and understand the areas where you may become vulnerable.

So, how is a strategy tool like SWOT analysis helpful for an author? This type of analysis will force you to examine your books and brand. It will provide an avenue for you to improve and grow.

Example:

Below is the SWOT analysis for this book, *Market or Die*.

Strengths:

* Written specifically for authors.

* Provides easy to understand, proven, methodologies and tactics for improving book marketing.

*Use of examples by published authors throughout the book.

* Information is timely and relevant.

Weaknesses:

* Appealing to a niche market could affect wide volume of sales.

* Not a quick hit. The book must be digested in its entirety to employ all of the methodologies into one plan to achieve success.

Opportunities:

* Book opens the door for in-person and online workshops and classes taught by author.

Threats:

* Many competitive titles about book marketing are already in existence.

* Some authors do not believe marketing is a necessary part of their job.

* The author teaches a discipline. Success is based on how well the audience understands the concepts and puts lessons into practice.

Throughout the development of the marketing plan for *Market or Die*, I capitalized on the strengths to increase the opportunities for book sales. I also understood the weaknesses to plan for and devise a communication plan to address threats and turn them into an opportunity.

SWOT analysis may seem simple to put into practice for a nonfiction work, but how would an author go about performing an analysis for fiction? Aspiring mystery author RM Lane submitted her SWOT analysis as an example for this book. In this analysis, the author has used SWOT to examine her book as well as herself as a writer.

In RM Lane's work titled *Fatal Image*, she lists a brief pitch for the book, and then performs her analysis below:

Fatal Image by RM Lane

A female former war correspondent living in exile in rural Kentucky horse country investigates the killing of a horse show judge when the clannish yet divided community comes together to accuse an innocent man of murder.

Strengths. Strong voice. Likeable sleuth narrator. Unusual protagonist—female former war correspondent. Book-of-the-heart passion. Immerses readers in setting. Twists and surprises toward the end. Inside view of a new subculture. Author makes commonplace sinister. Romantic subplot. Rich atmosphere. Author active on social media and blogging communities, and not afraid to network. First book in series.

Weaknesses. Horse world setting. Kentucky setting (not CA or NY). Setting a small niche breed of horse shadowed with controversy. Unknown author. Book-of-the-heart tunnel vision?

Opportunities. Sell at equine trade shows, equestrian competition venues, and tack shops. Kentucky also has a lot of book fairs, literary festivals, horse shows, and horse-related gift shops. Author has horse blog with growing readership and is quick to pounce on horse stories in national news.

Threats. Controversies shadow this niche breed. Lane has known equestrian enthusiasts to reject books featuring this niche breed no matter the topic. New author with more of a following as a nonfiction writer. Author not a speedy writer.

As Ms. Lane develops her marketing plan, she can use promotional tools such as targeted digital advertising and her strong networking skills to reach her fan base since her book would appeal to a certain type of reader. The horse breed featured in the book is known for controversy. Therefore, her work would only appeal to a specific audience. Because the audience is niche, she has also called out the many additional selling opportunities for this book at horse shows, tack shops, etc.

Ms. Lane has also detailed the weaknesses she foresees with the book. Should her book receive criticism, she is prepared and is in a position to make necessary corrections.

To assist in the creation of a SWOT analysis for use as a strategy tool, start by answering the following questions.

Strengths:

* What does this book deliver?

* What do you do better than anyone else?

* What can you offer the reader that will make them happy?

Weaknesses:

* What could you improve?

* What should you avoid?

* Are there any gaps in capability/knowledge?

* Is there anything that could impact your sales?

Opportunities:

* What does this book provide as a jumping-off point for the author?

* What can the author capitalize on?

Threats:

* What are other authors doing that you are not?

* What obstacles do/did you face with this book?

* Are there any changes/trends of note?

The results of your SWOT analysis will be used in the development of your integrated marketing plan. There are multiple uses for this analysis. On occasion, you may encounter feedback where a publisher isn't certain a particular work will sell in the marketplace. A SWOT Analysis is an excellent tool to perform to address this type of concern.

Author Landscape Analysis

It is fair to say most consumers who make a purchase do so using a process of evaluation. We often compare and contrast purchases with great rigor to ensure the best experience available. But, as an author, it's important to verify your marketing and promotional tactics are equal to your peers'.

In certain writing communities, authors do not like to think of themselves as competitors of one another; this is particularly true among romance writers. And, lucky for authors, there are enough readers to go around. However, to perform an author landscape analysis, it is important that you are able to identify likenesses within your own genre and sub-genre.

For example, you should answer the question: who do you write like? If a romance reader enjoyed a book by Tawny Weber, would they also enjoy a book by Adrienne Giordano? Maybe, but maybe not. These two authors write category romances for Harlequin, but the romances they write are designed to appeal to different audiences. While Ms. Weber writes high heat contemporary romance for Harlequin Blaze, Ms. Giordano writes for the romantic suspense line called Intrigue.

If you are unsure who you should compare yourself to, you should use the comparison tool on Amazon.com where it states, "Customers who bought this item also bought." You may want to compare yourself against those with the same publisher, or other authors you admire. The only constraint is to choose an author in the same (sub) genre whom you believe will share the same target audience.

By performing an author landscape analysis, you can evaluate yourself against your peers to identify any gaps in your marketing activities. The goal is to identify the gaps, then evaluate if you will need to add any money to the marketing budget to fill them. Performing the analysis is very simple—just rack and stack.

To begin, choose several authors in your same genre. Then, compare all of them to yourself. Examine each of the following:

* Do they have a website?

* Do they engage in social media? If so, what platforms?

* Do they use Quick Response (QR) codes? If so, where? How?

* Does the author offer a newsletter? How often is it distributed? Did you sign up to receive it? If so, what content/information does the author provide in the newsletter?

* What types of promotions does the author run?

* Does he or she donate to a charity?

* Does the author have a street team/fan club? Where do they reside (Facebook, Twitter, etc.) on social media?

* What conferences/events/signings do they have planned?

* Does the author blog? If so, where? How often?

* Does the author offer workshops, classes, or lectures?

* Does the author utilize Goodreads? Have a profile? Sponsor a giveaway? Advertise?

* Does the author have an Amazon page?

Collecting, then comparing answers between two or more authors for all of these marketing tasks can be daunting. However, if the results are captured in a table, the findings are easier to see. Below is an example from 2012/2013, where I performed an author landscape analysis for paranormal romance authors Molly Harper and Sara Humphreys. *Note: The authors have made changes as a result of this information. This is simply a working example of the end result of an author landscape analysis.*

Author Websites:

Molly Harper:
mollyharper.com

Sara Humphreys:
novelromance.net

QR codes:

Molly Harper:
No use of QR codes

Sara Humphreys:
QR code on blog is used to subscribe to newsletter

Newsletters:

Molly Harper:
Available newsletter, not easy to find

Sara Humphreys:
Available newsletter, not easy to find

Website Appearance:

Molly Harper:
* Home screen displays the following:
* Link to blogs
* Fun stuff and FAQs
* Upcoming events
* Character graveyard
* Press room
* Contact information
* Molly's latest book is front and center with links to Amazon.com
* Small Facebook and Twitter links, no feed integration

Sara Humphreys:

* Home screen displays the following:

* Slideshow of current and upcoming books with links to excerpts and video trailers

* Latest blog entry

* YouTube channel

* Encourages sharing via numerous outlets ("Sharing is sexy")

* Facebook, Google+ and Twitter widgets along the bottom of the screen

* Clean interface with short engaging messages about the books

Website (About Section):

Molly Harper: Updated bio describes Molly's transformation from aspiring writer as a kid to full-time author

Sara Humphreys: Bio page emphasizes Sara's education, interests, and other professional activities (Taney Speaker Training)

Website (Books):

Molly Harper:

Book covers link to Amazon

No summaries or excerpts available

Sara Humphreys:

Summaries, excerpts and video trailers are available for most books

Includes purchase links to Amazon, Barnes & Noble and Books-A-Million

Website (Contact):

Molly Harper:

Contact Molly via form (requires name, email, and security check)

Sara Humphreys:

Contact info available, form for rights information or interview queries

Website (Visitor Forum):

Molly Harper:

No forum or message board

Sara Humphreys:

No forum or message board

Website (Contest):

Molly Harper:

Most recent contest was to help promote her website

Prize: free books

Sara Humphreys:

Win signed ARCs by "liking" Sara's Facebook page

Website (Fun Stuff, Giveaways, Multimedia):

Molly Harper:

Link to Audible.com for audio books

Playlists

Character graveyard

Sara Humphreys:

Personalized Kindlegraph message

Free eNovella (Facebook)

No character information

Website (Photos):

Molly Harper:

All photos are book covers

Sara Humphreys:

All photos are book covers

Website (Events):

Molly Harper:

Events page lists blog tour and scheduled signings

Sara Humphreys:

Events page lists blog tour and scheduled signings

Website (Blog, Diary, News):

Molly harper:

Companion blog titled "Single Undead Female" and subtitled, "Nice Girls Don't Write Naughty Books"

Sara Humphreys:

YouTube channel

Sara's blog is full of photos, news, personal updates, and reviews

Website (Workshops):

Molly Harper:

Molly is available to book clubs via Skype

Sara Humphreys:

Taney Speaker Training

Website (Press Room):

Molly Harper:

Molly has a downloadable press kit complete with photos

Sara Humphreys:

No downloadable press kit

Social Media Presence (Facebook):

Molly Harper:

Yes

Sara Humphreys:

Yes

Social Media Presence (Twitter):

Molly Harper:

Yes

Sara Humphreys:

Yes

Social Media Presence (Pinterest):

Molly Harper:

No

Sara Humphreys:

Yes

Donation to charity?:

Molly Harper:

No information available

Sara Humphreys:

No information available

Have a "street team":

Molly Harper:

No

Sara Humphreys:

Yes, Sara's Angels

Actively looking for Angels around the country.

Online release parties:

Molly Harper:

No

Sara Humphreys:

No

Amazon Author Page:

Molly Harper:

* Utilizes Amazon Author page really well; it includes:

* Latest blog entry

* Latest tweet

* Author bio

Sara Humphreys:

* Utilizes Amazon Author page really well; it includes:

* Latest blog entry

* Latest tweet

* Latest Author video
* Author bio

Utilize Goodreads:
Molly Harper:
No

Sara Humphreys:
Yes—similar information to Amazon author page; Sara regularly engages with fans and followers on the site

Once you perform the detailed analysis, you can then make some recommendations for marketing tactics you can change or perform. Results from the above analysis provided both authors with the following suggestions to enhance their marketing:

Molly Harper

* Incorporate your blog into the webpage. This will create a better experience for fans. Going back and forth between sites can be confusing at times, and worse, some fans may only spend time on one or the other.

* Your blog is a great asset and should be featured prominently on the website.

* Great fan engagement on the blog with giveaways. Make these more prominent on the website.

* On the Books page, add synopses and information for each book. Currently, only the book covers are displayed. There is considerable empty space on this page, and adding excerpts or summaries would be a great use of the space.

* Convert your Facebook page to a Facebook Fan Page. This is a better way to engage fans on the site. It is also easier to see who is sharing your posts and who they are sharing them with (potential new fans!).

* Include book summaries and longer excerpts on your Facebook page. A good way to do this is use the Scribd app on Facebook (http://faceitpages.com/blog/how-to-add-a-scribd-document-to-facebook/759/)

* Incorporate the newsletter signup into the website (as opposed to emailing a request).

* Consider starting a "street team" to spread the word about your books.

Sara Humphreys

* You maintain a presence on the following sites: Facebook, Twitter, Tumblr, Goodreads, Amazon, and Pinterest. Recommend you create a hub on your website that makes these sites more apparent to fans and makes navigating these sites much easier.

* Convert your Facebook page to a Facebook Fan page.

* Include book summaries and longer excerpts on your Facebook page.

* Make branded merchandise available for fans via CaféPress.

* Consider using Google AdWords or Facebook Ads to drive traffic to your site.

* Change the URL to your primary site containing your name.

Without the implementation of strategy tools into your overall marketing plan, you will eventually find yourself boxed into a corner without the knowledge of what to do next with your promotions. Using strategy tools keeps you from wasting valuable time and money. It is important for you to spend the needed time thinking about your marketing strategy months to years before publication.

Key takeaways from this chapter:

* Strategy tools will help you learn where to spend your marketing budget, learn what the target audience expects, and justify saying, "no thank you."

* A positioning statement details what you expect to deliver to the reader and what result you expect from the delivery.

* A SWOT analysis is a simple tool for understanding your strengths, weaknesses, opportunities, and threats. SWOT analysis can be used for strategic planning, brainstorming, or decision making.

* An author landscape analysis is important for you to be able to identify missed promotional opportunities.

* The goal of an author landscape analysis is to identify promotional gaps and evaluate if any monies from the marketing budget will be need to address the gap.

Chapter Eight

Where the Plan and the Budget Connect

After completing the marketing strategy tools, you need a budget to move from strategy to execution. Assigning budget often gets over-looked. The temptation to simply plaster the message about your book anywhere and everywhere is too great. And, sometimes the budget you have, and the budget you need are vastly different. However, it is important for you to properly research the funding needed for your budget. This allows you to know the cost needed to effectively reach your intended audience. And, make decisions on where to cut funds if the budget becomes an issue.

To begin, you should analyze the results of the author landscape analysis to identify if/where there are any gaps in your marketing outreach. If you identify a need, you should examine costs required to fill the space and allow for it in the marketing budget. However, there is one thing you must have—a website. A website can be costly, but it is essential to your platform. In addition to the website creation and maintenance, you may also set aside monies for:

* Advertising placement (print, digital, or both)
* Advertising creation
* Website hosting
* Author photos
* Author travel
* Contest prizes for readers

* Book release parties
* Book trailers
* Freelance publicity (publicist) services
* Promotional items (bookmarks, pens, giveaways, et al)
* Social media (promoted posts, boosting posts, sponsored tweets, etc.)
* Fan club/street team rewards and supplies
* Mailing/shipping

A rule of thumb when building a budget is to research and add the cost for each item in the budget, then add 20% to the total. The added percentage will allow for and offset unexpected expenditures.

Example:

Below is an example of a marketing budget to promote *Market or Die*:

Advertising

Full page print advertising	$750
Ad creation	$80
Website hosting, per year	$300
Author photos	$ 300
Author travel (hotel, airfare, meals)	$2,000
Prizes	$50
Book release parties (in person)	$0
Book trailer/video	$900
Promotional items	$250
Publicity Services	$0
Social Media	$250
Fan Club	$200
Mailing/Shipping	$350
Total	**$4,930**
Add 20% (for unexpected expenditures)	$986
New total budget	**$6,416**

Not every author can afford to support every marketing and promotional opportunity for every release, which is why having the SWOT analysis and a completed author landscape analysis is so important. Using these two strategy documents, you have the ability to make informed decisions about where to place your available marketing dollars to best support the book.

This is the point in the budget where the hard decisions are made. Obviously, $6,400 in book marketing funds would be great to have if you have the money to spare. In this example, the strategy comes into play. Knowing the target audience, competition and strengths, weaknesses and opportunities, *Market or Die* can be promoted for a $900 investment.

Social media advertising and promoted posts	$300
Freelance publicity services, blog tour	$100
Travel, in-state writers' group meetings	$200
Book trailer	$300
Total	**$900**

You should research any/all free opportunities for book promotion. Some ideas for free book promotion are:

* Create a hashtag for your book

* Upload an excerpt of the book to Wattpad

* Encourage friends and fans to post reviews

* Host a Q&A session on Google+

* Leave your book name or website address on all voicemail messages

* Create/submit press releases

* Solicit radio show interviews

* Offer to join book clubs via Skype

* Post purchase links in your email signature

* Celebrate your book release with a Facebook release party (ask fellow authors to join in)

* Utilize Library Thing

* Submit articles to writers' associations

* Submit for a listing on addictedtoebooks.com

* Submit the book to be featured on Free Book Friday ◈

* Fill out the form for a free submission on Digital Book Today ◈

(◈ only if book is available for free)

It does not matter which promotional opportunities you engage in; your goal should be to focus on discoverability rather than sales.

Freelance vs. DIY Publicity

The purpose of this book is to empower you and teach you marketing so that you can perform all activities, from strategy to budgeting to execution, alone. However, for most authors, there aren't enough hours in the day to write, much less market. So, how do you know when to hire a freelance publicist vs. doing promotional work for yourself? The results of the SWOT analysis and the author landscape analysis can be a useful tool in predicting where you need assistance.

The goal of a freelance publicist is to provide the author with many different opportunities to promote the book. Publicists are not personal assistants.

Help from a publicist may be needed if:

* You are unable to nail down your brand.

* You hope to get the attention of the media. It is best to have someone act as an advocate on your behalf.

* You are remiss in having a social media strategy.

Other advantages for hiring a publicist are:

* Contacts. They know the publicity game, and how to get your book in the hands of the right people who will talk about it.

* Guidance. Many publicists help their clients avoid pitfalls and wasted time. Publicists also coach their clients before interviews, or provide guidance on how you should appeal to the reader. Publicists often perform website critiques and social media evaluations.

What questions should you ask yourself before hiring a freelance publicist?

* What are my goals for the book?

* What do I want the publicist to do?

* How could a publicist help me with my identified weaknesses?

Once you have made a decision to hire a freelance publicist, you should be ready to interview your publicist of choice. Like all relationships, a publicist/author relationship can be great or it can be a disaster for both parties. Therefore, I encourage you to properly research the publicist before hiring.

Questions you may want to ask the publicist are:

* How familiar are you with my genre?

* Do you have other clients within the same genre?

* Have you or would you like to read the book?

* What similar books have you publicized in the past?

* Do you have a client list?

* What are your areas of expertise?

* Can you supply a list of references?

* How long will I be supported once our promotional efforts have ended?

Note: There are differences between a publicist and a personal assistant. The responsibility of the publicist is to bring promotional opportunities to the client in the form of interviews, media attention, marketing strategy, et al to help the author gain attention for the book. Often, publicists do not manage your calendar, post on social media on your behalf, or create content for you to use for promotional purposes. It is wise for you to be sure of your needs before engaging with a freelance publicist to determine if you require assistance from a publicist or a personal assistant instead.

A credible publicist or publicity firm should be able to supply you with a list of references, testimonials from clients, and an explanation of the firm's cost structure. However, it is common for freelance publicists to be unable to provide samples of their work because this is confidential information which belongs to their clients.

Publicists are professionals. A strong author/publicist relationship will feel as though you have, at the very least, an advocate, and at most, a friend to help you with your publicity. However, not all publicists are created equal. It is important to understand how the publicist works. Some publicists specialize in a specific genre, while others have more contacts in the media. Therefore, it is essential that you know what type of work is needed prior to engaging with a publicist. Before you select a publicist, interview them. If their work ethic differs from yours, it is imperative that you and the publicist have a conversation to come to an understanding regarding the work flow. You should be concerned, how-ever, if the publicist fails to:

* Respond to emails or telephone calls in a timely manner.

* Communicate a plan as to how they will go about publicizing the book.

* Is too concerned about other clients.

* Engage in your own ideas regarding your publicity.

* Follow through on commitments.

If you are not satisfied with your freelance publicist, you should be familiar with how you can go about cancelling their services.

DIY Publicity

As stated earlier, this book in its entirety is designed to give you the tools to serve as both marketer and publicist for your work. Social media is the easiest tool for do-it-yourself publicity. The first rule of do-it-yourself publicity is not to focus on sales. Focus on discoverability instead. Too many authors will engage in book promotions once, only to not have it turn out the way they expected in terms of sales, and never engage in that type of promotion again. If you engage in marketing and promotion simply to focus on sales volume, you will be disappointed in your results every time.

What you should do is look at all book publicity as a learning experience; contacts you make today may not pay off until years later. To keep a writing career moving forward, the best thing you can do to market yourself is network.

In-person networking can be uncomfortable, especially for introverts. Coming up with topics for conversations with readers or with other authors can feel like a lot of pressure to someone who usually spends most of their time alone behind a computer. However, part of the success of your career is based on how well you network. Listed below are ten tips for in-person networking:

* Carry business cards at all times.

* Make eye contact when you are introduced; keep strong eye contact throughout the conversation.

* Use a strong handshake.

* Be sure to spend time listening and not monopolize the conversation.

* Arrive at events early.

* Set a specific number of people to meet during the event.

* Volunteer if an event needs help. If you are especially uncomfortable in social settings, volunteering gives you a "job to do" while interacting with others.

* Focus on building relationships, not sales.

* Follow up on requests, questions, or offers.

* Connect on social media post-event.

Just as there are in-person networking tips, there are also ways to improve your social networking online. Before engaging in social media, especially to build a readership or fan base, you should decide how much of your private/personal life you are willing to share. If you are aware of where the "line is drawn," you can have fun and be more relaxed in your communications. While there are many different social media platforms, below are tips for two of the more popular social media sites, Facebook and Twitter:

Facebook

* Like, comment, and share. If you are uncomfortable in social media, start slowly by liking, commenting, or sharing friends' information.

* Engage. Don't shy away from sharing bits and pieces about yourself.

* Think about your audience. What would help them get to know you better?

* Don't hard-sell. No one wants to be told to buy a book.

* Be yourself. Show your personality. Don't talk about books all the time.

Twitter

* Be helpful, interesting, or both. Twitter can be filled with a lot of nonsense. To network effectively, give your followers a reason to follow you. Passing along helpful tips or interesting information can lead to an increase in followers and retweets.

* Tweet about what you're doing. Find a way to put your own personal spin on commonplace activities.

* Use hashtags.

* Treat your Twitter profile like a business card.

* Like Facebook, Twitter is also not the place to hard-sell.

Do-it-yourself marketing doesn't stop with networking. Should you wish to take social networking one step further, you can run a campaign using the relationships you've built online and promote your posts. Promoting or sponsoring posts in social media requires use of your budget. However, a successful promoted post campaign can grow your contacts exponentially by providing you new readers to engage.

A rule of thumb for promoting posts is not to spend money for anything which will not gain you a return. (The definition of return means: sales, clicks, votes, newsletter subscriptions, number of likes, retweets, page views, et al.) Below is an example explaining how promoted posts can be successful:

In January 2013, my publicity firm participated in a contest. We wanted to spread the word to our fans on Facebook about the contest and ask for their vote. For an investment of twenty dollars, we boosted the post which told our fans about the contest and included the link for them to click to vote for us. Admittedly, we used the hard sell and asked for their vote since time was running out. Our normal Facebook fan base sits around 1,050 people; however, because we chose to boost the post, 5,500 people saw our plea for votes. Our firm took second place in the contest.

If you choose to spend marketing dollars on promoted social media posts, below are some tips to make the most of the experience:

* Offer up compelling content. Give the user a reason to comment, like, share, or retweet. If there's a deadline, let the audience know.

* Test the post first before paying to sponsor. Post the message, see if the post will "take off" organically. If it is not performing the way you'd like, adjust the post. Evaluate the way the post is written. Does it sound like a hard sell? If so, rewrite and try again before paying to sponsor.

* Ensure your call to action is clear.

* Use images. Images have a higher share ratio than plain text.

* Use available data. Evaluate the posts that are getting the results you are looking for. On Facebook, look at the Insights page to gauge the time of day or day of the week most fans are online; promote posts accordingly.

* Respond to all interactions. Responses keep the communication threads/tweets alive.

* Monitor the results.

* Have fun. Show your personality on all of your promoted posts.

Often, authors will ask if promoted posts are worth it. Did they just throw a piece of their marketing budget down the drain? Promoted posts do work, if you provide good, engaging content and think about what you are trying to gain from the promotion at the start. Promoted posts are about access. In the earlier example, the promoted post reached 5,500 people for an investment of twenty dollars. What is the likelihood that if you were in a room with 5,500 people, you would be able to reach each one and communicate your message? Maybe if you walked on stage in front of all 5,500 guests and addressed them with a microphone, you could have reached them all, right?

That is exactly what promoted posts are—reaching a vast group of people with a microphone, only virtually. And, just as if you stood on stage in a room filled with people, some would take heed of the message while others would ignore it. The same happens online. The investment you make to promote the post buys your (virtual) ticket to walk inside the room.

Key takeaways from this chapter:

* A marketing budget is needed to move you from strategy to execution.

* You should analyze the results of your landscape analysis to identify any gaps in your marketing outreach which need to be filled in.

* A rule of thumb when building a marketing budget is to add the costs for each item, then add 20%.

* Invest in discoverability rather than focus on sales.

* Freelance publicists are not personal assistants.

* Freelance publicists can help with media coverage, branding, building a social media strategy, making contacts, and offering professional guidance.

* If you wish to do your own publicity, do not focus on sales.

Focus on discoverability.

* Networking is important for authors.

* A rule of thumb for promoting posts is not to spend money which will not gain you a return.

Chapter Nine

Putting the Plan into Action

In this chapter, you will take the marketing strategy you have compiled and combine it with promotional efforts needed for execution. Here, you will build a marketing plan, assign promotional tasks, and list the timetable for completion of each task. This integrated plan will put strategy and execution steps together to teach you how they relate to each other.

Earlier strategy taught you how to identify gaps and where you should focus your promotional efforts. Below is an example of some of the promotional tools available to you, and the pros and cons of each.

Advertising (Print and Digital)

A paid space in the media dedicated to your book.

Pros:

* Digital advertising is an effective way to capture reader interest. In a brief ad, the reader can be directed to a purchase link or website to learn more about your book. Digital advertising offers the opportunity for you to obtain reports on the metrics of the activity to determine the impact and effectiveness of the campaign. Print advertising is a good tool for brand awareness.

Cons:

* Cost. Print advertising, especially in national newspapers and

magazines, can be extremely costly. Digital advertising is cheaper and ranges from the hundreds to thousands of dollars. Advertising is a broad, passive approach to finding readers.

Website

An Internet location which focuses on you, your work, and your brand.

Pros:

* All authors should have a website, even a basic one. A website is your "home base" on the Internet where readers can find all of the information about you and your work. Its advantage is that a website can be updated with relevant information as your career changes.

* It also provides a connection and education point for readers. A professional quality website instills confidence in the reader. It is a subconscious form of communication that lets readers know you plan to be around for the "long haul." Websites tell the reader that you take your job seriously. If the website is good quality, chances are, the books will be too.

* A website allows you to have a twenty-four-hour, global presence that can be accessed by anyone at any time.

Cons:

* Maintenance. It takes effort on your part to keep the website fresh and up to date. Whether you hire someone to maintain it or maintain the site yourself, chances are, you will be responsible for the content of the site. It may cost you money to keep the site reliably hosted and maintain a professional look and feel. However, this is a minor expense when compared to the overall value of your website.

Award Opportunities

Awards are given to books that stand out above others in their genre.

Pros:

* Submitting a book for entry into a competition can be a great way to create buzz about the book. If the awards allow for fan votes, this gives you an opportunity to rally your fan base to encourage voting. If the awards are judged by a panel or society, winning or finaling for the award gives you something to talk about other than "buy my book." Winners and finalists are generally publicized by the organization which provides an opportunity for some "buzz" about the book.

Cons:

* Cost. Some awards charge entry fees. Also, some awards only accept printed copies of manuscripts, which may mean mailing fees.

Conferences and Conventions

Many conferences and conventions offer networking opportunities, workshops, reader interactions, book signings, parties, and professional development.

Pros:

* Whether the event is reader-centric or author-centric, conferences and conventions offer a valuable opportunity to connect with others. Remember, connections made in person may not see a payoff for years later. However, that doesn't mean they're not important to cultivate. There are a vast number of conferences and conventions within the literary community. You should be able to find local events with a brief web search. A place to start is <u>readerevents.com</u>.

* Other advantages include educational opportunities and making face-to-face connections.

Cons:

* Availability. Many popular conferences, especially reader-centric conferences, are quick to fill. Therefore, conduct adequate research in advance so that you are aware of registration and reservation activity.

* Cost. Book festivals, reader events, and professional author conferences are expensive. Along with the cost of registration, you should expect travel charges and personal expenses in addition to any books, prizes, and promotional pieces you wish to give away to prospective readers.

* No guarantee. Your participation in a convention or conference doesn't guarantee an increase in readership.

Press Kit

A press kit is a package designed for the media which contains your press release, pitch for the book, photos, and suggested interview questions, etc.

Pros:

* Simplicity. An electronic "kit" can be housed online and made available for members of the media to download.

Cons:

* Usage. The author can put a lot of time and effort into creating and updating their press kit, only to find it is rarely used.

Promotional (Giveaway) Items

A piece of merchandise printed with the author's brand.

Pros:

* Many items including bookmarks, pens, and coffee cups can be labeled with your brand. These promotional items can be used anywhere. Promo items are used in every industry because they help to communicate brand and increase brand awareness. The best you can hope from the use of a promo items is that it will entice the reader to discover you.

Cons:

* Cost. While some publishers can provide you with promo items, most of the cost sits with you. I encourage you to buy in bulk to offset expenses. Also, there may be little to no return on your investment. Rarely do you know how well certain items "worked" at events. I encourage you to purchase items of use which will lend themselves to being kept rather than thrown away post-event.

Book Signing

An event where authors engage with readers to sign books, perform readings, and/or answer questions.

Pros:

* Connection. Book signings provide you with the opportunity to connect with readers. The bookstore or book festival will promote the appearance. These events give you an opportunity to spend a bit of personal time with readers and bond with them. Often, signings will include readings from the book, which also provides fans the opportunity to ask questions. Signings also provide an opportunity for new readers to become exposed to you and your work.

Cons:

* Participation varies. Ill-timed or poorly promoted events can yield low participation rates, therefore not making it worth your time.

* Cost. Travel costs are generally at your expense.

* Materials. Some bookstores do not stock independently-published titles, making it more difficult for you to hold a signing. E-book signings have come a long way. With downloadable apps (such as on authorgraph.com), signing an e-book has become less awkward. However, there is still a struggle to "fill the void" when a physical copy of the book does not exist.

Blog Tour

A virtual tour to assist you in promoting your book, which is held on the Internet, usually on various reader blogs, book review sites, and other book-centric websites.

Pros:

* Blog tours allow you an opportunity for brand recognition, especially if you are a new author. Blogs which have a strong, engaged readership can achieve sales for you. Popular blogs get you noticed. And blogs also leave behind a "digital footprint" for you so that readers can return days, months, or even years later to find a specific post. Most bloggers are a valuable resource. They know their readership, and they can provide you with assistance regarding what type of posts the audience prefers.

* Cost. If you choose to schedule your own blog tour, you will incur no cost.

Cons:

* Balance. Writing unique, individual posts for each blog on

the tour can be exhausting. Too many blogs, and you begin to repeat yourself; too few, and you will barely make a dent in book promotion.

* Contacts. You may not have the proper contacts to schedule your own tour and therefore will need to seek assistance.

* Expectations. You may expect too much from a blog tour. Instead of viewing the tour as a vehicle for book promotion, you may judge the success of the tour based on the number of responses a blog post receives or sales based on an appearance on a blog. The blog tour is only one part of a collection of tools used in book publicity.

* Repetitiveness. To a large degree, blog tours can begin to feel as if you are only reaching the same readers/blog followers. Often, the same people seem to be on all of the blogs, not to follow authors, but looking for prizes.

Fan Clubs/Street Teams

A group of super fans who promote the author, their books, and their brand in the marketplace.

Pros:

* The creation of fan clubs or street teams can be thrilling. These devoted readers will be the first to read, post reviews, and spread the word about the books and authors they love. Without the support of their street team, many authors would not have advocates spreading the word about their books, both in person and online. Street team members have been known to rearrange bookstore shelves, putting their favorite authors at eye level. Their "job" as a street team member is to share their excitement about your book. When given advance copies of books, street teams can begin discussion forums or post re-views on sites devoted to books, like Goodreads. Healthy, ac-tive, devoted street teams can carry you for years to come.

Cons:

* Commitment. Like all things created, if you expect your fan club to flourish, you (or your publicity staff) must maintain it. Finding the time to adequately support the team while writing (especially when you are between releases) and promoting

existing titles can seem daunting, and it is not uncommon for unmaintained street teams to go stale and lose their luster. Once this has happened, it's often difficult for you to put the team back together, and it is also damaging to your brand. Why? Fan clubs are typically comprised of your super fans. And, if you do not maintain the team and allow it to go astray, you are essentially letting your core fan base down.

* Cost. Should you provide materials or giveaways to the club, this is generally performed at your expense.

* Control. The street team is an extension of your brand. You must realize that you are responsible for controlling your street team. Therefore, if a member responds angrily to a negative review or violates any "team rules" set by you, you will need to address such behavior.

Newsletters

A communication vehicle (electronic or print) which can be used to pass information from author to reader.

Pros:

* Easy to execute. Offering a reader newsletter can be a valuable asset for an author. By having the reader subscribe, you can capture the reader's email address and use it for other promotional efforts.

* Cost. Most newsletter services are either free or inexpensive.

* Opportunity. An author newsletter can provide insider information or special offers to your subscribers.

* Increases awareness. You can encourage your readership to share or forward the newsletter in social media which increases your reach.

* Measurable. Most newsletters services offer measurements—open rate, click-through rate, bounce backs, and number of unsubscribers are important metrics for you to track.

Cons:

* Maintenance. Newsletters should be distributed on a regular basis. You can define the term "regular," but it is important that you stick with your commitment to provide the infor-

mation the reader is looking for. If there has been a delay between newsletters, it's appropriate for you to address it. Keep in mind, it may take you some time to find a schedule that works best.

* Content. Some authors struggle for newsletter content. However, the good news about newsletter content is that shorter newsletters that include links generally perform better than longer newsletters. If you find yourself without much to say, use images or maybe give a brief personal update.

Direct Mail

A traditional direct mail campaign is when a piece of marketing material is mailed to a physical address (most commonly called junk mail).

Pros:

* Direct mail campaigns work because, with the rise of email communications, the number of pieces of physical mail has fallen. Therefore, recipients are more apt to look at each piece received.

Cons:

* Cost. Mailing costs for physical pieces of marketing materials, especially those not of standard size, can be costly.

* Low response rates. Unless some type of code is placed on the piece to use for redemption, measuring the effectiveness of a direct mail campaign can be difficult.

* Environmental. It is likely that direct mail pieces will be thrown away, which impacts the environment.

Reviews

An advance copy of the book may be supplied to book bloggers, fans, or the media who will provide an honest review of the work.

Pros:

* Credible. Book reviewers are some of the most respected opinions in the industry. Readers follow reviewers, and their opinions matter. You can promote a positive review on social media, your website, and inside your other books. Positive reviews get attention by media outlets. A scathing or negative

review can also have a positive impact on sales (yes, it's true!). Any reviewer who mentions your name and the book's title is a "win" for you.

Cons:

* Some reviews contain spoilers which can impact the book's sales.

* If your book does not receive any reviews, this may be detrimental to your success.

* With the high number of books hitting the market and the review requirement some advertising venues have, reviewers are often backlogged, making reviews harder to get, especially timely reviews that tie in with other marketing efforts.

Contests

Contests are offered to engage readers in an activity to win something of perceived value.

Pros:

* Contests can be a fun, interactive way to promote both book and brand. Contests can be used as a vehicle to capture other reader information, such as email addresses.

* Buzzworthy. Offering a contest provides you with something besides the book to talk about in social media. Contests can create buzz in the marketplace.

* They have the potential to go viral. Photo/Video/Essay upload contests are the most engaging type of contests because they require something from the participant. Sweepstakes contest are the most passive form of contest entry, requiring the least maintenance and the least amount of engagement.

Cons:

* Rate of return. No one can predict the response rate for a contest. Contests have been bastardized over the years and have caused people to believe they never win anything. The more work required on behalf of the entrant, the lower number of entries you should expect. Whereas, the less amount of work required of the entrant, the potential for spam increases.

Using various types of promotion helps you to keep momentum going behind your book. Do not be afraid to "mix it up" or try something new. As listed above, pros and cons exist for every promotional vehicle. None of them are perfect, but when used in conjunction with a solid marketing plan, they can help give your book the lift you are looking for.

With multiple promotional vehicles defined and the pros and cons examined, you can then begin to put the marketing plan together. The following should be displayed as part of your marketing plan:

* Your goal

* Your brand statement

* A detailed description of the target audience

* The positioning statement

* A completed SWOT analysis

* A completed Author Landscape Analysis, with gaps identified

* A listing of promotional efforts to address identified gaps

* New or repeat promotions

* Itemized budget

* Timetable for execution

You should view the listing of promotional efforts as the wheels which keep the momentum for the book rolling. Promotions should be staged so that they occur pre-release, during release, and post-release. Some promotional activities, like social media, will be used in each stage. Note: Some promotions are dependent upon items such as ARCs (advance reader copies) or cover art to be supplied by the publisher.

Following is an example of the order in which promotions may be executed. However, there are no hard and fast rules.

Pre-release (six months or earlier)

* Website creation and hosting

* Author photos taken for press kit and website use

* Confirm participation/register for space at conferences, conventions, and reader events.

* Submit to award opportunities

* Reserve print advertising space

* Decide which social media platforms to participate in and

begin engaging

* Write your author biography

Pre-release (four months before)

* Organize street team/fan club

* Create and order promotional items

* Reveal the book's cover art in social media

* Encourage pre-orders on social media if links are available

* Reserve digital advertising

* Solicit reviews from book bloggers

* Organize blog tour and online appearances (allow twelve weeks)

Pre-release (two months before)

* Contact local booksellers, introduce yourself, and set the stage for a signing

Pre-release (one month before)

* Start "talking up" your book in social media

* Craft all marketing messages for your street team to communicate

* Mail promotional items to street team for distribution

* Engage heavily in social media

* Organize a contest

A few weeks before

* Send out press release materials and media pitches

* Set up signings

* Kick off the contest

* Begin media interviews

Release Day

* Promote the release in social media

* Celebrate with an online or in-person release party

* Conduct media interviews

Post-release

* Wrap-up contest and communicate with the winners

* Wrap up media interviews
* Encourage readers to review the book
* Promote positive reviews in social media

Romance author Dani Collins shares her opinions on a sample timetable for her marketing and how she's learning to make marketing work for her.

"I'm still working on perfecting my Book Launch Plan. I would love to have a firm system, but I'm still test driving different strategies.

"A year ahead, I might be thinking about how one title can tie into an existing book, but things are very nascent. My lead time with Harlequin is usually around nine months from acceptance to publication. When they give me a title, I tweet it. At that point, I make some decisions on things like contests, swag, blog tours, giveaways, etc., and assign some deadlines.

"With Harlequin, there is a fairly predictable pattern for receiving certain materials. When I receive my blurb, cover, and author copies, I post them to Facebook or incorporate them into blog posts, and send the art for bookmarks, etc.

"Six weeks ahead of the print launch date, I run a month-long giveaway on Goodreads. I also start a six-week series of #SampleSunday blog posts with 1,500–2,000 word excerpts from the beginning of the book. I add buy links to these posts along with links to the Goodreads contest and often link to other posts or books in the same series. Often I run a Facebook ad to promote at least one of the posts in these series (the first or last one) and tweet several times through the week with the link. I am typically on blog tour at this point and post the links to my guest posts on Twitter, Facebook, and within these #SampleSunday posts.

"I'm actively working to build my newsletter list. I include the subscription link in my bio on all blog tours, etc. The newsletter comes out on launch day and I always have a winner of one signed copy of the book. I post the link to the newsletter on Facebook and Twitter and have boosted that post to increase reach.

"I haven't yet tried a Facebook launch party, but will soon. I also want to try a Goodreads ad. I don't yet have a street team. It's on my radar, but it's such a huge commitment, I want to be sure I can maintain it. I have done signings, have written articles in the *RWR*, and I regularly attend various conferences, which all help with general exposure, but they're not part of my routine launch plan."

Frequently asked questions when building and executing a marketing plan

Q. Do I have to create a marketing plan for each release?

A. No. However, you should create a marketing plan so that with each additional release, you can update it to include the most relevant information. Over time, you will learn what works for you and what does not. Book marketing and publicity has a lot of moving parts. A marketing plan is a mere guide to keep your momentum headed in the right direction.

Q. Do debut authors need street teams/fan club?

A. No, a street team or a fan club isn't a "must have." In fact, you shouldn't create a fan club unless you are fully committed to support it for a very long time. However, some authors have a voracious readership. Those authors should harness the reader's excitement and put their enthusiasm to work for them.

Q. What do I do if I receive a negative review?

A. Remain professional. Do not respond negatively or have others respond negatively on your behalf. Remember, a review is simply one person's opinion. There are plenty of books that reviewers have hated, but readers couldn't get enough of.

Q. What are some mistakes authors make in marketing?

A. One of the biggest mistakes you can make is to wait to begin your marketing efforts. You cannot start marketing only weeks before a release and expect to be successful. Brand theory teaches that a consumer must interact with a brand three times before they will take the leap of faith to make a purchase from an unfamiliar brand. Waiting too long to begin promoting the book means that you have shortened the time between those interactions, and have missed out on opportunities to connect with buyers.

Also, with the rise of e-book publishing and independent publishing, some authors have shifted their focus from quality of books to quantity of books. Remember, as an author, having a well-written book is the best form of promotion for your next release. Self-published books should offer the reader the same quality of editing, cover art, and storytelling as traditionally published books. Throwing a book out onto the market that is poorly edited, has a lesser quality cover, or lacks in storytelling damages your brand.

Q. How does an author recruit a street team?

A. Start by corralling the "super fans." These are the people who email you and rave about the book. They are also the ones who post reviews when you ask them to. Ask them if they'd like to be a part of the group. To grow the team, it's important that you decide what the team "rules" are, and what's required of the participant. Communicate these rules either via website or social media group. Then, put the call out for team members, but do so by saying that they need to perform an action (like emailing you) to become a team member.

Many times, authors will put a call out on social media to recruit for their street team. This may lead people to become part of the team for what they can receive, not necessarily on what they will give back. By asking the prospective team member to perform an action (like sending an email), you are essentially knitting them into the group, trying them out, evaluating them to see if they'll do as you ask. If the participant isn't motivated enough to send you an email declaring their interest to become part of the team, you shouldn't expect that that person would visit their local bookstore on your behalf.

Q. Where are other places to advertise my book besides Facebook?

A. The list of sites who offer digital advertising for books is endless. Here are examples of a sampling: Shelf Awareness, Reddit, Bookreporter.com, CriminalElement.com, Smartbitchestrashybooks.com, Heroesandheartbreakers.com, readerevents.com, freshfiction.com . . . and many others.

Q. What is the appropriate length of an author biography?

A. Because you never know how the biography will be used, I advise you to have both a long and short version. The shorter version may be comprised of one or two paragraphs and is used mostly in the media. The longer version should be three to five paragraphs. If you are holding a speaking engagement, workshop, reading, or teaching a class, the organizers will typically ask for a longer bio.

Q. How much of my personal life should I divulge to my readership?

A. You should think about your social media policy. What are you willing to share? Where's the line? Some prefer to be as private as possible, while others are an open book. Then, there are those who land somewhere the middle. Discuss with your spouse or significant other what they feel should be kept private, and honor their feelings.

Q. How is a press release written?

A. The words FOR IMMEDIATE RELEASE should appear in all caps at the top left of the page, above the headline. This is followed by your name, phone number, and email address (if you are submitting the release yourself). Next, the headline will appear in bold, capitalized letters, followed by the sub-line. The headline and sub-line must be eye-catching and newsworthy. If you have trouble creating the headline, ask yourself, why does the reader care? Put the most relevant information about the book in the first paragraph. Keep the release short, no longer than two pages. Proofread for correct spelling and grammar. Refer to yourself by your last name, without a title. For example, "Fusco writes how-to marketing books for writers." Make sure to properly "end" the release, either by using—end—or ###. Include all contact information including website address, links to social media, email, phone number and physical address.

Q. I can't "toot my own horn." How can I market myself?

A. The good news is, marketing isn't bragging. So, you won't have to toot your own horn. Knowing if you are an introvert or extrovert will help you tailor your marketing activities and help to make you feel the most comfortable in promoting the book. And, when you feel comfortable, you can be successful.

If you are introverted, you may naturally gravitate to more

online marketing. Activities such as social media engagement, advertising, blog tours, and contests can all be executed without facing the reader in person. If you are more comfortable behind the screen of your PC, think about hosting an online party, chat, or workshop to promote the book. Email newsletters are also an effective form of communication.

If you tend to be extroverted, in-person book signings, readings, and events are where you will shine. Blog Talk Radio interviews are an excellent choice for the extroverted author, as well as volunteering and social media engagement.

Talking about your book isn't tooting your own horn. It's expected. If you share your excitement, the feeling will become contagious.

Q. What does an example of a high-level marketing plan look like?

A.   There's no hard and fast rule to the amount of detail needed for a marketing plan. Essentially, what they are asking you for is a list of marketing and promotional ideas without going into too much detail. Sometimes, these high-level plans are used to accompany proposals. If you have an agent, you should probably work with your agent to confirm how much detail is required. For example, I also write fiction. Below is an example of a high-level marketing plan I submitted along with a book proposal for a contemporary romance titled *Stolen Hearts*.

Marketing Plan—*Stolen Hearts* by Jennifer Fusco

Tagline: She stole his wallet, he stole her heart.

Short-Term Goal: Build brand recognition and readership in contemporary romance.

Long-Term Goal: Publish in both long and short contemporary romance.

* Amazon Top 100 Author

* *USA Today* Bestselling Author

* *NYT* Bestselling author

Target Audience:

Women aged 30-54, primarily located in the South who read both on an electronic device and in print. <u>RWA Reader's survey</u> reports 57% of readers are willing to try a new author.

All of Fusco's characters are deeply flawed and have a humorous twist. Adult contemporary romance readers who enjoy Carly Phillips, Rachel Gibson, and Jennifer Crusie may also enjoy Fusco's work.

Promotional Activities:

As the owner of a freelance publicity firm, Ms. Fusco has the access, ability, and plans to complete the following:

* Reach out to over fifty bloggers for reviews and blog tour opportunities
* Send out press releases and pitch local media
* Participate in readers' conferences (*RT*, etc.)
* Advertise in digital and print
* Develop a book trailer
* Create and distribute monthly newsletter
* Conduct a promotional contest
* Send email campaign to readers
* Heavily engage in social media (Facebook, Twitter)
* Continue bi-monthly column for RWA's *RWR* to build brand recognition
* Seek out endorsements from author friends and clients
* Host book signings, readings

Ms. Fusco's first nonfiction book, *Market or Die,* a how-to marketing book for writers, will be released from BelleBooks in 2015. She expects additional pull-through sales of her fiction title based on the release of her nonfiction work.

Key takeaways from this chapter:

* An integrated plan puts strategy and execution together.
* Build a launch plan and assign a timetable to your promotions.
* Plan and execute post-release promotions.

Chapter Ten

Circle of Influence

How to Entice, Engage, and Reward a Readership

Authors are constantly searching for new ways to expand, entice, engage, and reward their readership. In marketing, growing an audience is sometimes called widening your sphere of influence. It's a fancy title for a simple theory. Take a look at the graph below.

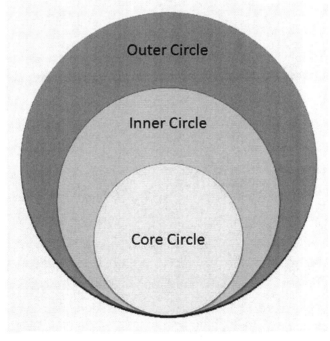

The core circle represents the people in your life who know information before anyone else. Core circles often include your family, friends, agent, and super fans/fan club. The inner circle represents the second tier of relationships you make. This may be bloggers, reviewers, and members of the press, other authors, convention organizers, and readers and "friends" in social media. The third circle, the outer circle, represents people who know of you, but you fail to know them. These are the people who purchase your book, form an opinion about it, and tell others, but never engage with you. Scary, huh?

Your task is to leave a lasting, positive effect on these readers. But how can you accomplish this, especially when you don't even know them? To succeed, you must grow your inner circle by continuously challenging yourself to meet new people. To some authors, this sounds overwhelming, especially since writing is a solitary profession and not all writers are comfortable putting themselves out there. However, there are ways to widen your sphere of influence and produce positive word of mouth without having to become the life of the party. It starts with two words: creating awareness.

Luckily, most authors are readers, too. So, it isn't difficult to step into the shoes of today's book buyer. By drawing upon our own experiences, we can paint a picture of what today's reader encounters when trying to find a good book and understand their challenges. Challenges for today's reader are:

* Competition. Millions upon millions of choices, with more authors and books entering the publishing world every day. How does a reader choose?

* Varied pricing. E-book prices range from free to the double digits, depending on the publishing house or, if independently published, the price set by the author. How much is the reader willing to pay?

* Inconsistent quality. Traditional publishing houses have allowed books to release with uncorrected errors. These same grammatical errors can be found in self-published titles. It's not unheard of for an author to have three or four beta readers go through their book, yet they still find errors. Quality matters. Will a reader try your books again if they are riddled with errors?

* Fear of the unknown. It takes a leap of faith for a reader to

try a new author. While some genres are more welcoming than others of debut authors, there still remains a bit of a risk on the part of the consumer. Why should they try your book?

* Access. As an author, you shouldn't assume every reader owns a tablet or e-reading device. If you're releasing in e-book only, how will the print buyer hear about the book? How can you help the reader find your book?

Finding new buyers means that you must widen your inner circle. To widen your inner circle, you start by creating awareness. Creating awareness starts with answering a few simple questions:

1. Who are you?
2. What do you do?
3. How can you help?
4. Why should anyone care?

When you answer these questions, then you can create a combination of your answers to provide an answer to this:

5. How do I add value?

The term "adding value" refers to what the members of your inner circle will find important or useful about your message. Here, you determine what your inner circle wants and then provide it. When an audience reads a message that they deem valuable, this lends itself to creating word-of-mouth buzz. Then, you use the promotional tools you've become familiar with (blog tours, social media, advertising, etc.) to enhance the created buzz. This is important because it will aid readers in finding you.

Here is an example of how I widened my inner circle.

Expanding an author's sphere of influence isn't a summer project. It spans the length of the author's career. I started out giving a marketing presentation about brand to my local writing chapter in 2010. It was a skill I had that I didn't know others needed to learn. My chapter mates were so impressed by the presentation, they recommended I submit a proposal to speak at local chapters and national writing conferences.

Had I not listened to their suggestions, I would probably not have enough brand recognition to be signed by BelleBooks to write a marketing book. I had a skill, a talent, which made me more "valuable" than the romance writer I intended to be when I joined my local writers group,

CTRWA, in 2010. However, I haven't stopped writing romance.

Speaking engagements and online classes led to guest blog opportunities, and additional brand recognition. All of that "attention" led to opening a publicity firm in 2012. From there, I've held my own one-day marketing summits.

Sure, widening a sphere of influence is about meeting people, but it's more than handing out a business card. It's about letting your audience know what you do well, and building on it over time.

I believe the worst thing you can do is judge your success or failure on numbers alone. For example, if you have a thousand Facebook fans, and believe you are more influential than someone who has five hundred, this is simply not true. Or, that if you have ten thousand likes, you must be reaching people. Eh, not necessarily. It's only true if all of those ten thousand people are truly engaged, which is doubtful. Yes, you should employ measurement and analysis, but by no means are measurement and analysis the judge and jury of successes and failures. I've made connections throughout my career, and those connections may not have paid off until two years later. In marketing, that's how it goes.

Most authors I know aren't a patient lot, and we're all a little bit neurotic and want to see immediate results. That's not going to happen, at least where growing your inner circle is concerned. However, if, as authors, we make a concentrated effort to show our value to our readership/target audience, the circle will widen organically over time. And it's not only natural, it is sustainable.

Below are a set of best practices when working to widen a sphere of influence.

* Ask how. A common mistake is for authors to ask why this book or that book did not sell. Or, why do you not have as many friends or blog opportunities or attention as someone else? Instead, you should ask how you can create your own opportunities. The more original and creative the idea, the better, because it's likely no one else has tried it.

* Turn problems into opportunities. While the advice sounds cliché, it is not. Consider what problems or issues your audience members face. Bringing forth solutions to problems helps not only in their resolution, but brings you brand recognition and attention at the same time.

* Communicate your skill set. Other than writing, what are some other skills in your wheelhouse? You can incorporate these skills into your writing life and career to teach others.

* Maintain the right attitude. People are more likely to connect with those who are upbeat and positive. Connecting people to other people is a great networking tool that will pay off as these connections grow. If you attend a networking event or reader convention, you must leave your problems at the door and be the brand.

Once the inner circle grows, this expansion will also affect the outer circle. Again, the outer circle is comprised of people who know your brand, but do not interact with you. The easiest and fastest way to widen your outer circle is to produce the best quality books possible. Great books are infectious. Thoroughly satisfying reads get readers talking. Extraordinary books have the ability to pull readers from the outer circle to the inner circle.

But, the efforts don't stop there. If you are interested in expanding your outer circle, you should invest both time and money in the following: research, social media, editorial, and word-of-mouth buzz.

Research

With a few keystrokes and Internet searches, you can perform a basic search which will give you information for finding your target audience. Using the Internet, you can search for demographic information. Knowing who your target audience is can determine how and where this audience spends their time and their money. For example, if you want to target the teen market, you may research spending patterns in teens. If you can determine where and how a teenager spends their money, you can also brainstorm how you can put your books in front of that audience. If teens spend a small percentage of their paycheck or allowance on books, and the largest share on food, how might you capitalize on this knowledge? How can you get your book in front of your target audience where you know they are spending money?

Maybe you should advertise in cafés, food courts, and other eating establishments that attract teens. However, you must be mass-marketed for this to work effectively. You could also seek out endorsements from food or beverage products which target teens. Here is where research results can help you spawn new marketing ideas to help attract you target market. When you are informed and create ideas rooted in fact, the possibilities are endless.

The Pew Research Center offers free statistical and sociological information. Companies such as Pew Research Center, Bowker, and Ingram often produce useful, statistically driven articles about the publishing industry. If you don't have time to research their websites in depth, follow the aforementioned companies on Twitter.

Blogs are also a valuable tool for gathering anecdotal information. Blogs generally express opinions, not statistically proven facts. Therefore, you should perform additional research if you are solely making a decision based on blog research.

Social Media

Creating awareness is about people reaching people. Social media sites such as Facebook, Twitter, Google+, LinkedIn, Instagram, Pinterest, and Vine help authors reach new people. It is not necessary for you to splatter yourself around social media. In fact, the more proficient you become with one platform, the more successful you will become. Almost all social media sites allow you to create groups, advertise, and connect. Below is a brief introduction to some of the widely utilized social media sites.

Facebook: With roughly 500 million users, Facebook is the most popular social networking site. To access Facebook.com, you must create an account on the site which is free. Facebook users must be at least thirteen years old. Facebook is good for author networking because the site allows for personal pages, fan pages, advertising, and creating groups and events.

MySpace: On MySpace, the first step is to create a profile. Then, invite friends to join and search for friends already profiled on MySpace. These contacts become your initial Friend Space. Once the friendship is confirmed, all the people in your friends' Friend Space become part of your network. In that sense, everyone on MySpace is in your extended network. MySpace users must also be a minimum of thirteen years old to register. Per the terms and conditions of MySpace, users who are thirteen to seventeen may be restricted.

MySpace is one of the oldest social networking sites. The average age range of MySpace users, according to AdAge.com, is fourteen to twenty-four. This information may be useful for you to connect with younger audiences.

Twitter: Twitter allows the user to communicate to their network in one hundred and forty characters or less. With a Twitter account, you can build a network of contacts by following others and inviting others to receive tweets. You can also send followers a direct message. Twitter makes it easy to opt in or out of networks. Additionally, the user can choose to stop following a feed.

LinkedIn: LinkedIn doesn't focus on making friends or sharing media such as photos, videos, and music. Instead, it promotes professional connections. To start using LinkedIn, the user must register and create a profile page. Personal information is required. With this site, you can update your profile with relevant details and a summary. Additionally, the site allows for professional endorsements. According to their website, "LinkedIn operates the world's largest professional network on the Internet with more than three hundred million members in over two hundred countries and territories."

If you are trying to grow your network by promoting your skills and educational background, you can utilize LinkedIn for this purpose.

Vine: Owned by Twitter, Vine is a mobile app which allows users to create six second video clips and distribute them via Vine's social network or to the users' Facebook and Twitter feeds. Vine may be useful for authors because it has the ability to visually communicate a marketing message to readers.

Wattpad: Wattpad is a social community which allows users to share stories and connect. Currently, the site boasts twenty-five million users and growing, and is 85% mobile across all devices. According to Wattpad's terms, "you will not create an account if you are younger than thirteen years of age." Wattpad allows writers to upload and share their stories to grow an audience.

Editorial

The definition of editorial, for use in growing the outer circle, is twofold. If you choose to independently publish, it is paramount to seek out editorial assistance to produce the best quality product. As mentioned in previous chapters, a poor quality product can and will damage your brand.

For the purpose of widening a circle of influence, you are encouraged to apply the same editorial scrutiny to messaging. You must also consider using an editorial eye when crafting social media messages or advertising to capture new readers. You must look at your messaging critically and determine how it will sound to a reader who has never heard of your work. Ask: Is the message attractive? Will the audience understand it? What does this message say about me and the brand? Continually revise messaging to eliminate any confusion.

Buzz

It is important for you to remember that growing a circle of influence includes more than an analysis of numbers alone. Yes, most promotional tools such as social media, advertising, contests, newsletters, etc. do include a form of measurement and analysis. But, when growing your outer circle for the purpose of bringing audience members into the inner circle, while also expanding limits of the outer circle, you can't accurately measure all activity. The most important element to expanding the outer circle is word-of-mouth buzz. Buzz cannot be measured in hard and fast numbers.

But you have two attributes to your advantage which can supercharge word-of-mouth buzz: creativity and interactivity.

You are encouraged to measure where you can, but also be conscious to add adequate time to allow the circles to grow and buzz to spread. Women's fiction author Kim Boykin explains her attempts to widen her circle of influence during her promotion of her book, *The Wisdom of Hair*.

"Everybody thinks writing a book is hard; it's not. What nobody tells you, but you find out fast when you have a book to sell, is that competing against literally millions of books for sale through Amazon, Ingram, and other booksellers feels a lot like trying to whisper to someone on the other side of Times Square and hoping to be heard. As a newbie, I invested in my writing career, spending money on necessities like a new website, advertising, visiting book clubs, even if they only had three or four members. I hired a publicist, had a myriad of promotional materials like bookmarks made, and held giveaways for gift baskets and books. I put every dime from my advance back into my first novel, *The Wisdom of Hair*, and then some.

"Not everybody has money to put into their publishing career, but whether you're self-publishing or going with one of the Big Five, unless you get a huge advance, you're going to have to spend some money. The average advance these days from the big time publishers is $4,000, and believe me, it does not go very far.

"So what do you do if you don't have money to invest in your career? You make friends, lots of them. Where do you find these friends? At conferences, online, in writers' organizations, and critique groups. You help them every chance you get, and ask them to do the same when the opportunity arises. If you're a good copy editor but don't have a clue about social marketing, or you blog consistently but can't tweet to save your soul, find someone who would benefit from your skills and trade off.

"One reason self-publishing is a great option for aspiring authors is you can actually make some money to put into your career, provided that you produce a good, error-free book with a great cover, and you market said book. For instance, if your book is on Amazon, you get 70% of your sales.

"I'd considered self-publishing romance to build audience. With romance readers accounting for 80% of fiction sales and the fact that they are voracious readers and happily cross genres, it was a good idea. And I wanted to make some money. I thought self-publishing was the answer for me, but I ended up at a small press writing novellas. They produce great covers. All I do is spend time writing and engaging in social media. Unless you get a huge advance, a small publisher will outperform the big ones because they have fewer books to market and can give each release the attention it deserves. I'm not saying all small publishers are created equal, but I am extremely happy."

Social media and networking may be more important to those authors who do not have the support and distribution provided by a publisher. Independent publishing sensation A.M. Madden writes sexy, rock-and-roll romance stories. An avid reader turned author, Madden learned firsthand how important social media and social media networking was going to be to her career. With hundreds of reviews on each of her three books in the Back-Up series, Madden quickly mastered social media. She writes:

"Let me begin by saying I have a love/hate relationship with social media. I recognize that it is necessary, but at the same time, I find it can be extremely distracting, and unfortunately takes up way too much of my time. I'm approaching my first anniversary since I hit that publish button for Back-Up. A year ago, besides writing the book, hitting publish was the only other task I had completed. In hindsight, I most definitely made mistakes. Building a following and a fan base, is exhausting and a lot of work. Doing so after a book is released is even more so. I've often said writing the book is the easy part. After publishing Back-Up, I thought to myself, 'Okay, now what?' I quickly found I was chasing my own tail.

"I reached out to some of my favorite authors for advice. The authors that I reached out to were fantastic in responding with some great tips and advice. I followed each and every one of their suggestions. First thing I did was to join Goodreads and added my book. Slowly, readers began adding it to their TBR lists. Slowly, I acquired ratings and reviews. The first five star review I received, I did a happy dance.

"A few months after I published, I hadn't made much progress. It was frustrating to watch my followers creep up a few at a time, wondering what I should do to get myself noticed.

"Once Back-Up was out there, I spent days upon days contacting bloggers, requesting them to read and review my unknown little rock star romance. Most ignored me, but some were very supportive and took me under their wings. I developed relationships with these bloggers, who are now considered some of my best friends. These blogs took an unknown author, such as myself, and promoted me. They posted their reviews and 'pimped' me for no other reason but because they loved Back-Up.

"My next task was creating an author Facebook and Twitter account. I needed a lesson in Twitter from my sons. I had no idea what I was doing. When I hit a hundred followers on Facebook, I gave away a copy of my book to celebrate. I then purchased a domain name and spent weeks building my website. Again, all of this was necessary, but also very time-consuming when trying to write book number two while working full-time.

"I began doing takeovers on blog pages. I met some fantastic readers who told their friends and so on. Some of them are still on my street team and are my friends as well. In a year, by adding more books to the series, and working my social media pages every day, I now have more than six thousand followers on Facebook. I have one hundred and thirty members on my street team. I've hit the Amazon Top 100 in Overall Kindle Books, and have been maintaining top 100 in my Romance Genre categories for all three books. I hit top 10 Best Reads on Indie-Author

News. I hit top 25 in Smashwords Best Reads in the Romance Category. My characters have their own following, with my main character Jack Lair having his own fan club, Facebook page, and Twitter account. Blogs are now contacting me for takeovers.

"With the many authors vying for 'pimp' time and the many book boyfriends competing in blogger contests, branding becomes an important tool for an author trying to develop a following. A unique logo, a must-have swag item, or a quirky hashtag are necessary tools in social media game we all play daily. Sending a fan a signed bookmark, or a rubber #LairLover bracelet speaks volumes when developing a fan base. Selling signed paperbacks, T-shirts, mugs, or novelties bearing your logo on do-it-yourself Internet stores such as CaféPress, all help to boost that brand even more, and are invaluable tools in becoming a household name in your genre.

"Did it come easily? Absolutely not. To this day, I dedicate several hours every morning to do my 'social media routine' as well as several hours every night. I share my buy links in groups to help promote my books. I respond to every single reader that pms (private messages), emails, or tweets me. I schedule at least three to four takeovers a month, interacting with any reader who attends. I read every Facebook notification where someone suggested my books or posted on my page. I interact with my street team with fun facts and questions of the day. I've gifted many copies of my books, my swag, and gift cards.

"It's a constant effort and a specific mindset that is absolutely necessary. The distraction can be harmful when I am trying desperately to finish a book and Facebook keeps calling, but it is all still necessary."

The Importance of Blogging

One of the greatest misconceptions you can have is to believe blogging is not valuable. A second misunderstanding common among authors is that blogging doesn't generate sales. If you believe either of the previous statements, you are encouraged to look at blogging through a different lens. Adopting any one of the two beliefs above can work against you if your goal is to widen your circle of influence. There are many arguments to support why you should blog. Three reasons are listed below:

* Drives traffic to websites. Should a reader or industry professional happen upon a blog containing a well-written, insightful blog post, you stand a better chance of capturing the interested

reader and leading them to your website. This interest begins to draw them into your outer circle. Over time, the reader first attracted by the blog moves from the outer circle to the inner circle. Other tips on how blogging drives traffic to websites may include: the use of keywords and phrases, publishing consistently, networking or linking to other blogs, and adding share buttons to the blog.

* Brand Recognition. Blogging provides the opportunity for those unfamiliar with you to understand your brand and where you fit in the marketplace. If the reader chooses not to engage with you at the time of the blog, blogging plants the seed in the mind of the reader. When the reader encounters you or your work a second or even third time, you are not foreign to them.

* Develops relationships through interaction. Should the reader choose to leave a comment on the blog, they are letting you know that they are open to establishing a relationship with you. You should respond to all comments, letting the reader-ship know their inputs are valuable and appreciated.

Someone who believes in blogging is urban fantasy TOR author Suzanne Johnson:

"I began blogging in November 2005 while living in New Orleans and trying to rebuild after Hurricane Katrina. I had a daily blog (weekdays) called 'No-No-NOLA' that was basically a place for me to vent all the anger and sorrow and frustration. I kept it up until I left New Orleans in late 2007. Blogging had already become a habit for me, plus I worked as a journalistic writer and editor so, again, blogging was a comfortable fit.

"When I sold my first book in 2010, I started a blog because that was expected, but I had no idea what to blog about, and it languished while I navel-gazed. My 'business plan' for 2011, while I waited for that first book to come out, was to write another book and to either get serious about my blog or ditch it. I was mostly being read by other authors, and I knew I needed to attract readers, first and foremost.

"Since I was writing primarily paranormal, I decided to go after the paranormal reader. I knew one way to initially draw people in was to give stuff away. So that's what I did. I gave the blog a name (Preternatura) and branded it by clearly defining what types of material I would run and that I would post five or six days a week. I featured new speculative fiction books, particularly in my genres of paranormal romance and urban fantasy, and started conversations about paranormal fantasy and fiction. I began to use Twitter at key times of day to drive traffic to the blog. It grew slowly but steadily, and I recently published my 2,000th post.

"Blogging has allowed me to build a community of regular readers—not just for the blog, but for my books. It increases my visibility. Maybe the most important thing it does is keep my name at the top of the search engines (pushing me ahead of the wife of the New York Jets and the former director of Goldman Sachs, both also named Suzanne Johnson). Now, if you search my name on Google, all the links on the first page of results, and at least half of the second page lead to my blog or to my books.

"Is blogging for everyone? Probably not. It's time-consuming, and if you're going to get your blog noticed among all the other blogs out there, it takes a concerted effort. But blogging is a comfortable space for me, and a way for me to have conversations with readers in a way that I can't with Twitter or Facebook because of my work schedule (full-time day job and full-time novelist). If an author can't think of anything to say beyond promoting his or her book, is writing primarily about writing, and doesn't want to commit to posting frequently, it's probably not the right marketing platform."

Additionally, Harlequin Love Inspired author Katy Lee began blogging before she was published, and she's found group blogging more successful for her. Her blog, "Writing Secrets of Seven Scribes," rotates blog posts by each group member which are designed to engage with the same audience. Ms. Lee writes:

"You've worked hard to write the best novel for your readers, but did you know it's just as important to write to your readers as it is to write for them? Having an online presence with a blog is a must for any writer desiring to be successful in their career. Blogging can be a reward for your readers and a way to grow your followers. By offering an online gathering place where they are welcomed and valued, where they are treated with a backstage pass to you personally, you have an opportunity to take your career to another level just by talking to your readers. Yes, I said, talking to. If you want to establish yourself as a successful author, you must talk to your followers. You must stop thinking of them as the faceless button-pusher who bought your book, and see them as members of your own personal club—members who are your ambassadors to their own sphere of influence, and who just might have friends who would like to belong to your club too. Your followers are the key to your big success story.

"Now, I know there are a slew of blogs out there, many with little to no hits. So, what are the different factors at play for the big hitters? First off, these bloggers know who their readers are. This is nothing new. You've known since you began writing that understanding who your readers are is crucial. An agent wouldn't look twice at you if you didn't know what market you were writing for. Well, visitors to blogs are the same way. They know right away if a certain blog is written for them in mind, or if they've happened upon a strange land that they don't belong in. If a viewer decides they are in a comfortable place, they may choose to browse further to see if you are writing to them in particular. What they see in the first minute (or less) will be the deciding factor of whether or not they stay or go. What they shouldn't see is a blatant push to buy your book.

"As much as you want to go for the big sell, readers need to see the value of buying your work. The best way to do this is by including them in the process of your story-making. With your blog, show them insights into your research. Humanize yourself and share about your mishaps. Involve them in your learning curve, ask them for advice, and take their comments seriously when they give them. I recently read an article about a highly successful clothes designer that found her following just by asking people their opinion on her designs. Things they liked, things they didn't. Colors that grabbed them, or shades that faded into the background. People don't want the hard sell in their face, but they do genuinely want to help you. Give them ample opportunity to do so, then show them your gratefulness with little rewards. They love to be recognized, so don't forget to do this. Rewards also keep them coming back to your site.

"A concern many authors have about blogging is a lack of content to blog about. If you are including your readers in the process as I stated above, you shouldn't have to worry about this at all. If you are paying attention to their comments and posts, you should always have material to write about. Keep track of topics that matter to them and ideas that are a concern. Now, you have a blog topic. And if the situation warrants it, reference them as a key player in your post. Then watch the shares and retweets spread far and wide.

"I do want to clarify one thing about blogging for an author. I know I said you should never go in for the hard sell, but blogging is only going to be beneficial to your sales if the readers know you have books to sell. This is a tightrope you need to balance on well, because every post should lead readers to your stories in some 'soft' way. Make them laugh with your mishap during research—the research needed for a certain scene in the book. Now they have to know how it turned out. Pull on their heartstrings about a character's plight that is real to your readers because they can relate, and they will feel a connection to your book—and want it. Design your posts to show the benefits of having your book on their shelf, and they will buy it and tell their world about it. But, none of this can happen if you're not blogging."

Engage and Entertain in Social Media

Openness in social media is attractive to others, and it is important to your growth that you remain engaging, and sometimes entertaining, online. You must first gauge the personality of your social media audience as a whole. Determining an audience's personality is guesswork and takes a great deal of trial and error. By posting different types of communication, you are able to gauge if the audience likes humor or to be serious. Do they prefer educational information? Photos? Etc.

Contemporary romance author Kelsey Browning found the way to her audience's heart by asking them their preferences. She often posts questions such as, mustard or mayonnaise? Paper or plastic? And her audience goes wild. She's learned the personality of her readership on Facebook. They like to share their preferences and be heard. Ms. Browning entertains her fans by providing them the opportunity.

However, not all audiences will respond to paper or plastic with such zeal. Some readers prefer a more conversational approach. *New York Times* bestselling historical romance author Eloisa James provided an account of how she engages her audience:

"I have a large Facebook page, with over 71,000 fans. I also have Pinterest boards, a Tumblr account, and a Twitter account. The secret is to multi-function, and don't do much of what you don't like. I really love Pinterest and Tumblr for their own sake—I'm fascinated by all the creative imagery I see. Those are labors of love, which I enjoy as much as anyone who happens to follow me. Maintaining a Facebook page is an art. We all know how difficult that is—but it's an art that you need to command, with the market as it is.

"I engage my Facebook audience by sharing things I enjoy as an author, reader, and a mom. Updates about my teenage daughter are quite popular right now, and I often talk about the romance novels I'm reading. My Facebook and Twitter pages are pretty much my version of a circle of girlfriends who are voracious readers. We all love to talk books!"

As stated above, Ms. James monitors what posts are popular among her fan base, and what topics they find engaging. She knows her audience likes to talk books, therefore she provides them the opportunity for book discussions.

Rewarding Loyalty

Airlines have frequent flyer clubs, credit cards offer points rewards, restaurants sometimes offer free food, but what can an author do to reward loyalty? While an author doesn't have the resources that corporate America does to reward loyalty to consumers, options do exist for rewarding reader loyalty.

* Free reads. Offering a free story to readers is a great way to reward a loyal readership and attract potential new readers at the same time.

* Book discussions. Host an in-depth chat about your book which will give the audience an opportunity to ask questions and provide feedback.

* Crowdsource. Survey the readership and ask them what kind of topics they'd like you to write about. For fiction, crowdsourcing to brainstorm character names is a popular way to reward loyalty.

* Behind the scenes look. Share such information as character family trees, author playlists, character graveyards, trivia, photos, character interviews, and book or character inspirations.

* Downloadables. Provide bookmarks, trading cards, recipes, patterns, etc.

* Bonus Content. Post novellas, epilogues or prologues online.

* Mail-aways. Provide collectible cards/covers, or bookplates signed by the author.

Rewarding reader loyalty should be as important as writing. Why? Because interacting with your fan base and keeping them engaged, especially between releases, helps keep your brand in the mind of the reader.

Author Ted Fauster writes science fantasy. The genre is a hybrid of fantasy fiction and science fiction. His books are big, bold, and very quest-oriented. He heavily interacts with his fans on Facebook and Twitter. To promote his book, *Deomans of Faerel,* he created Facebook pages to promote his books, reward his readership, and keep his audience engaged between releases. He says:

"Keeping your readership constantly engaged is critical. With every sale, you bring someone new into the fold, into your family. Each person becomes indelibly connected to you, and whether you feel you have the time for them or not, your readers most certainly feel you have the obligation.

"The best way I've found to stay engaged is through social media. The infrastructure is already there; why not take advantage of it? This doesn't mean you have to personally engage with everyone who has ever purchased anything. That's just silly, and more than a little condescending. Rather, just pay attention. Use the 'lists' function on Twitter, click 'get notifications' on Facebook. Watch from afar. When you can, jump in and comment, just as if you were at a dinner party. Politely inject yourself into the conversation. Don't be shy. You'll be surprised how many genuine friendships develop. And that's what you're really trying to do with your writing anyway—connect with people—right?

"Facebook is still a biggie for me. I'm on all the time, which is easy with a smartphone. There's really no excuse to not pay attention. To increase my footprint, I build a page for every project I'm working on, whether it's finished or not. In fact, I started all my pages way early so that I could condition my followers to what's coming down the pipeline. For my World of Faerel series, I created a 'world' page as well as individual book pages for *Deomans of Faerel* and *Hellion King of Faerel.* I'll soon start a new page for *Conquest of Faerel,* which I've barely started writing. I find this builds a kind of snowballing interest and anticipation.

"But I don't stop there. I spend time on each of these pages, just as I do my author page, and 'like' things, 'share' things, and 'post' things I feel expose the flavor of that particular book. Over time, this builds momentum. One page feeds interest in the next. I always put the most emphasis on the next book to come, since that serves a dual purpose. Consequently, all associated pages benefit, and my readership grows as they come to learn more about each world. Readers feel empowered to do their own research—pulling that info from your pages. In the process, they get to know you as a writer and look forward to talking about each new thing you create. This 'word-of-mouth' phenomenon has to happen organically, and this is the best way I know how."

Enticing, engaging and rewarding a readership is an ongoing process. And, it is important for you to remember that anything you start (like a blog, for example) must be maintained. Should you feel overwhelmed, consider joining forces and partnering with a fellow author. This would allow both of you adequate time to be both promoter and writer without feeling as if you've abandoned your readership.

Key takeaways from this chapter:

* Growing an audience is sometimes called widening a sphere of influence.

* The sphere of influence is made up of the core circle, the inner circle, and the outer circle.

* Challenges facing today's book buyer are: competition, varied pricing, inconsistent quality, fear of the unknown, and access.

* Best practices when working to widen a sphere of influence include: asking how, turning problems into opportunities, communicating your skill set, and maintaining the right attitude.

* As the inner circle grows, the outer circle will also expand.

* Expanding the outer circle takes both time and money. Both should be spent on social media and editorial, with the intention of generating word-of-mouth buzz.

Chapter Eleven

The Ups and Downs of Social Media Marketing

If you are not involved with some type of social media marketing to build relationships, you are missing an opportunity. This chapter will take a deeper dive into social media to discuss the pros and cons of selected platforms so that you may choose the networking sites which you feel are best suited for you. To prelude this chapter, I interviewed social media expert Kristen Lamb. Ms. Lamb worked in international sales before transitioning into a career as an author, freelance editor, and speaker. She takes her years of experience in sales and promotion, and merges them with almost a decade as a writer and editor to create a program designed to help authors construct a platform in the new paradigm of publishing. Kristen has helped hundreds of writers find success using social media. Her methods are responsible for selling hundreds of thousands of books. She has helped all levels of writers from mega-selling authors to self-published unknowns attain amazing results. All writers are encouraged to visit her website: authorkristenlamb.com.

Q. In your opinion, what are some of the pros and cons of social media?

Ms. Lamb: "We are living in an amazing time to be a writer, and social media is a lifeline to cultivate a fan base (or even future fan base). Without a brand, an author is dead in the water. Brick-and-mortar bookstores are experiencing record contraction and shelf space is finite. Even if an author is fortunate enough to have her book in a bookstore, there are severe limitations.

"First, prime real estate (end caps, tables, displays) are generally VIP. Most first-time authors will be spine-out on a shelf. This means browsing roulette is the best she can hope for unless readers are specifically searching for her book. Additionally, books are only on the shelves for a specified amount of time. After that time has expired, the covers are torn off (for mass market paperbacks) and unsold inventory is returned to the publisher. If an author has multiple books for sale, odds are that only the most recent will be in a bookstore. The problem is, novelists make most of their money from compounded sales (backlists). This is why authors can make more money now than ever before. Digital space is infinite and doesn't expire.

"Thus, the pro of social media is that we can create relationships with people all over the world, from home, and for free. Most consumers, in a world of infinite choices, will buy from who they know and *like*, first. If those in our following enjoy our book(s), they can become our strongest evangelists and a powerful word-of-mouth selling force.

"In a sea of books, those voices can direct others to our book(s).

"If an author chooses to avoid social media, then she is competing against all of those who are using it well. This leaves the author vulnerable and dependent on luck, which is rare and fickle, or on traditional media, which is diminishing in importance. The mega-author isn't created by mobilizing avid readers. The mega-author is created when the person who might only read a couple of books a year becomes a fan. That fat part of the bell curve of individuals who buy one to four books a year is the hardest to mobilize, but once we get them going? A force of nature.

"Yet, these types of consumers won't read book reviews in journals, rarely go to bookstores, and don't read about authors in the newspaper/magazines or watch them on TV or listen to them on the radio. Why? They're on Facebook and Twitter. Also, they don't define themselves as 'readers,' so the content is not nearly as interesting as that YouTube video of kittens.

"The con of social media is that we, as authors, have to find a way to blend being a person and a professional, and that's a tough balance to strike. The Internet is forever. What takes years to create can take only seconds to destroy. An angry tweet. Too much political ranting. Negativity. All of this can create a negative brand. Yet, when sitting at home in jogging pants behind a screen, we can fail to be vigilant over what we post, and that can be costly.

"Social media done well takes time, work, and patience. A brand/platform doesn't appear out of the ether. Additionally, consumers today want authenticity, so outsourcing doesn't work. In fact, outsourcing can be resented. This means additional duties for the author. I hear a lot of, 'I just want to write the books.' Don't we all? This is a business. Considering that before the digital revolution, authors had roughly a 93% failure rate, I will take the additional work any day.

"According to BookExpo America, in 2006, 93% of all authors (traditionally and nontraditionally published) sold less than a thousand books. Of all traditionally published authors, only one out of *ten* ever saw a second book in print.

"One con that is pretty big is that social media is a double-edged sword. While it brings out the best in people, it can also bring out the worst. Faceless bullies hiding behind avatars and fake names abound. We must develop a thick skin and a network of supporters. We also have to *know* how to shut down bullies and learn not to feed the trolls.

"I've encountered authors who ended up on the wrong end of a gang of mean girls or bullies and gave up writing (and the bullies won). This is why it is *so* critical to have a community of support. When we encounter those types of people who spread misery just to spread misery, often our community will come to our aid and help shut down those who've gotten out of control. The rest is simply about us not taking it personally."

Q. How does social media benefit the reader?

Ms. Lamb: "Social media helps readers because it makes the mountain of choices manageable. They can connect personally to an author, and might even learn to love a genre they would have never before read. But, because they like the writer so much, they will step out of their normal reading patterns and try something different.

"We saw a similar phenomenon with iTunes (paired with social media sites like MySpace). When music lovers had to drop twenty dollars on an entire album, they stuck to the types of music they liked. When the paradigm shifted and consumers could buy a single song for ninety-nine cents, they were more apt to try new things. As a result, music lovers of today are far more eclectic.

"The same thing is happening with books. They are affordable, easy to access, and people are discovering new writers all the time in large part because of social media."

Q. In your opinion, which social media platform (Facebook, Twitter, Pinterest, etc.) should an author have?

Ms. Lamb: "I feel a blog is the most important (and ideally hosted on the author's website). With a blog, you *own* your content. The blog has survived since the 90s and won't go away, whereas social media networks come and go. Also, search engines will never direct someone surfing the Internet to one of our clever tweets or Facebook posts, but they *will* guide people to our blogs (where our books can be for sale in a very non-spammy way).

"Beyond the blog, Facebook and Twitter. I call it the Trinity of Social Media.

"Facebook moves slower. Posts remain visible for a longer period of time. Also, Facebook is great for harnessing the power of our close connections. Aunt Tilda who once criticized you for wanting to write, could eventually be your best salesperson. She might not read vampire books, but anyone in earshot who mentions needing to find a new book, she will likely try to convert.

"For instance, I switched high schools five times, and only connected to the place I graduated. People who never said more than three sentences to me twenty years ago now follow my blog, buy my books, and tell everyone they know me and to get my book even if they aren't writers.

"Facebook also allows for deeper relationships to build in both directions. Readers see us as people and as friends, and that word means something. We might initially connect off recipes we post or gluten-free food or yoga, but *then* they find out we write, too.

"Twitter is ideal for directing traffic to a blog or even a book (though be careful—no one likes book spam). Twitter is ideal for making content go viral simply because it has unparalleled power of amplification. We no longer are reaching people linearly (those in *our* network) we are reaching out exponentially.

"If we know how to properly use hashtags, Twitter is excellent for finding regular people who might read our books and for breaking out of the writer's circle. For example, if we write military thrillers, follow #Army or #Navy etc. and those hashtag groups are filled with military people chatting (who aren't writers but could be readers).

"We can also use hashtags to connect with experts to assist with the writing. Want to know how to use firearms properly in a novel? Use #AR15 and ask for help. Want to learn more about forensics? Try some salient hashtags. People are extremely generous, and experts are particularly generous. They *want* to help writers get the facts correct."

Q. Is it advantageous for an author to blog?

Ms. Lamb: "Extremely. Blogs will remain until the Internet goes away and when that happens? We have bigger problems than book sales. Search engines are super blog friendly and I gain new followers and fans daily from posts that are *years* old."

Q. For an author, should these platforms be used for relationship-building or as sales tools?

Ms. Lamb: "Stop selling. People are tired of it. We can't go anywhere that some ad or contest or promotion isn't jammed in our face. I believe we need to be balanced. Talk to people. Be interested in *others* first. *Serve* first. Sow good stuff and harvest will come. Yet, conversely, don't be shy. Writers *need* to tell people they have a book for sale or a new book coming out. They can mention contests or promotions or giveaways. Most sensible folks understand this is our living. When talking about our book/writing becomes counterproductive is when that's *all* we talk about. People either tune it out or resent the barrage of self-promo.

"I use the analogy of Rotary. Rotary International is a service organization comprised of local professionals. I was a member for almost seven years. We met weekly, had lunch, listened to a speaker, and did service projects together. We all knew what everyone did—accountant, financial advisor, dentist, veterinarian—but no one had to 'sell' us. When I needed a doctor, I went to the one in my Rotary club. When I needed an emergency vet visit for my dogs, guess who I called? All of these 'sales' were generated as fruit of relationships. Same with writers on social media."

Keeping all of Ms. Lamb's sound advice in mind, you are encouraged to educate yourself on all relevant social media platforms for audience engagement. Listed below are the most popular social media platforms, their mission, and the pros, cons, and usefulness for authors. You can select which medium may work best for you.

Facebook

According to Facebook's Facebook page, the company was "Founded in 2004. Facebook's mission is to give people the power to share, and make the world more open and connected. People use Facebook to stay connected with friends and family, to discover what's going on in the world, and to share and express what matters to them."

Pros:

* Easy to use.

* Fast.

* Post has the potential to go viral.

* Allows for the creation of groups and events.

* Promotes interactivity.

* Accessibility.

* Linking accounts allows for distribution of posts from other sites.

Cons:

* Easy to get "sucked in" and lose track of time.

* Timeliness of posts. Not all friends/fans see newer posts at the same time, if at all.

* Cost to boost posts or advertise.

* Hackers. Accounts can be hacked or hijacked. Frequent monitoring is needed to protect your account.

* Depression. It is easy to make false assumptions of perceived success or failure based on the number of responses, likes, comments or mentions to a post. If you feel too pressured or distressed by the interactions (or lack of) Facebook activity, you should ask yourself if this platform is right for you.

Facebook Do's and Don'ts:

Do: Have a positive attitude, keep it to your personality, and ask people to perform an action for you.

Don't: Rant, be political or polarizing, make instructions too complicated, or brag.

Usefulness for Authors:

* Readers "hang out" on Facebook.

* Newsletter registration apps integrate nicely with Facebook.

* Targeted advertising can help to drive traffic to a webpage.

* Events pages are useful when hosting an online book release party.

* Can drop in/drop out of conversations.

* Allows the posting of images.

* The book cover can become your profile picture.

* Allows for targeted advertising.

* Free, if you choose not to pay for boosting posts or advertising.

* Can add widget to blog or website.

Twitter:

Incorporated in 2007. According to Twitter's company profile, Twitter's mission is, "To give everyone the power to create and share ideas and information instantly, without barriers."

Pros:

* Unlimited number of followers, no limitations.
* Fast, gets to the point of the message quickly.
* Massive, global interaction.
* Accessible/Mobile.
* Can promote others via retweet.
* Can customize your profile page.
* Can promote tweets for wider reach.
* Life of a tweet is approximately four minutes.
* Uses hashtags to "label" conversations.
* Can target message to specific people using Twitter handles.
* Can post widget to blog or website.
* Tweet with the purpose of being retweeted.
* Follow anyone who follows you.

Cons:

* Busy/Crowded—sometimes hard to get attention.
* Character limitation.
* Costs to promote tweets or advertise.
* Hackers. Frequent monitoring of account your account can hinder it from being hacked.
* Addictive. Twitter can become a drain on your personal time.

Twitter Do's and Don'ts:

Do: Follow back, tweet often, promote your blog, connect with others, retweet your friends, and respond to messages.

Don't: Pitch sales all the time, obsess over the numbers (retweets, followers, favorites), or brag.

Usefulness for authors

* Excellent tool for widening a circle of influence.

* Reader can follow without feeling the pressure to engage.

* Fast—great tool for "spreading the word."

* Great for networking and promoting fellow authors via re-tweets.

* Can add widget to website or blog tour.

* Promotes sharing.

* Tweets can be scheduled (via Hootsuite or other scheduling medium) so that you can plan tweets in advance.

* #FF is Friday Follow. The goal is network building. Tag people and suggest to your audience to follow those people (only on Fridays). Example of Friday Follow tweet: #FF @authorsara, @jamiekswriter, @tlcosta, @TawnyWeber

* Aim to have more followers than people you follow. To trim your list, subscribe to: justunfollow.com

LinkedIn

Founded in 2003. Per LinkedIn's website, "Our mission is simple: connect the world's professionals to make them more productive and successful. When you join LinkedIn, you get access to people, jobs, news, updates, and insights that help you be great at what you do."

Pros:

* Establishes professional online resume.

* Establishes credibility among network via "endorsements."

* Global Access.

Cons:

* For professional use only. Does not lend itself to conversation or photo sharing.

* Time to create profile and manage endorsements isn't as important as writing or connecting with a readership.

LinkedIn Do's and Don'ts:

Do: Be professional, join in and participate in groups, and keep your profile current.

Don't: Spam, tout connections you don't really know, or worry about the numbers (quality over quantity).

Usefulness for Authors

* Nonfiction authors are encouraged to fill out an online profile via LinkedIn to establish credibility in their field through connections and endorsements.

* Authors who are interested in public speaking or teaching could benefit from a professional profile.

* Promote the "other skills" you can offer besides your stories (copywriting, editing, critiquing, or professional services).

* Network with other industry professionals who maintain LinkedIn profiles.

* Join a Group. Members can join groups and subgroups of like-minded individuals with common interests.

Vine

Per Vine.com, "Our goal is to provide a service that allows you to discover and receive content from sources that interest you as well as to share your content with others. We respect the ownership of the content that users share and each user is responsible for the content he or she provides. Because of these principles, we do not actively monitor user content and will not censor user content, except in limited circumstances described below."

Pros:

* Ease of use.

* Mobility.

* Creativity.

* Focused messaging—messaging must be no longer than six seconds.

* Reach/distribution—share via Facebook and Twitter by linking accounts.

* Vine is relatively new (debuted in 2013) and is owned by Twitter, which positions itself for growth potential.

Cons:

* Adoption. Established in January 2013, Vine needs time to establish itself among social media users.

* Time restrictive. Creating six-second looping videos can be challenging.

Do's and Don'ts for Vine:

Do: Use a narrative format for video content, only convey one point per video, and use audio.

Don't: Over-post, or try to fit too much into six seconds.

Usefulness for Authors

* There's great potential in creating a six-second looping video for book promotion, then using Twitter and Facebook to distribute the message.

* Use popular hashtags such as #unPOP, #magic, #StopMotion, #loop and #AllNaturalVines to ensure other community members view the video.

YouTube

"Founded in February 2005, YouTube allows billions of people to discover, watch, and share originally-created videos. YouTube provides a forum for people to connect, inform, and inspire others across the globe and acts as a distribution platform for original content creators and advertisers large and small."

Pros:
* No fees.
* Potential to go viral.
* Globally recognized and accepted.
* No time limit for videos.
* Can set up a personal YouTube channel.
* Can embed videos on websites.
* Ability to tag.

Cons:
* Little control.
* Cost may be incurred to produce a professional, high quality video.
* Distractions—users may get sucked in to cat videos instead.

Do's and Don'ts for YouTube

Do: Play to your strengths, collaborate with other YouTube channel owners, and tag videos.

Don't: Ignore feedback, over-promise, or publish all of your videos on the same day.

Usefulness for authors

* Can create and distribute videos, lectures, or book trailers with no time limitations.

Pinterest

Created in March 2010. "Pinterest is a tool for discovering things you love, and doing those things in real life. Ben Silbermann, Evan Sharp, and Paul Sciarra co-founded our site in March 2010. Since then, we've helped millions of people pick up new hobbies, find their style, and plan life's important projects."

Pros:

* Good for visual communication.

* Targeted audience—studies suggest 80% of Pinterest users are female.

* Attractive and easy to use.

* Repinning content expands its reach.

* High traffic site.

Cons:

* Not widely used by men. Could be difficult if the book targets a male audience.

* Privacy and copyright concerns. See Pinterest terms of use.

* Less conversational than other sites.

Do's and Don'ts for Pinterest

Do: Repin other people's content, comment on other's pins, share your content, and create new boards.

Don't: Pin anything and everything, or repin images that aren't sourced properly.

Usefulness for Authors

* If you are soliciting a female audience, Pinterest may be the place to look.

* Allows you to bond with followers using other interests besides books. You can pin pictures of your hobbies, interests, etc.

* Use Pinterest as an engagement tool. Create a board for your hero or heroine. What would he or she eat, drink, wear? Where would they go on vacation? What would their pets look like?

Instagram

"Instagram is a fun and quirky way to share your life with friends through a series of pictures. Snap a photo with your mobile phone, then choose a filter to transform the image into a memory to keep around forever. We're building Instagram to allow you to experience moments in your friends' lives through pictures as they happen. We imagine a world more connected through photos."

Pros:

* Many users, approximately two hundred million.

* Site appeals to the younger demographic.

* More personal.

* Encourages image and video sharing.

* Created for mobile use.

Cons:

* Limited integration with other social media sites.

Do's and Don'ts for Instagram

Do: Treat Instagram like an advertisement, give behind-the-scenes looks, utilize before and after shots, and hold a contest.

Don't: Overuse hashtags, post too often, or leave your profile unmaintained.

Usefulness for Authors

* If you are trying to appeal to a younger demographic, try Instagram.

* Can distribute photos via Facebook and Twitter.

Authors Sound Off

For the creation of this book, various authors were solicited for their opinions on what social media platform they prefer and why they believe it works for them. The goal is for you to understand that there is no singular tool or methodology for making social media engagement successful. Being effective in social media, and choosing which platform to use, is as unique and individual as the authors themselves.

Tina Wainscott: "I like Facebook because you can post pictures right there, which I like to do. And you can have easier interaction with readers."

Lorie Langdon: "I prefer Instagram because it's where I get the most interaction with teen readers."

Lane Heymont: "I like Twitter more because it's limited to 140 characters, so there aren't long drawn-out blocks of texts to read, and we are able to keep our private lives private. Also, I think it's easier to interact and reach more people."

Anna Hamilton: "It's a tie between Pinterest and Instagram! I love pictures and seeing everyone's creativity!"

Dani Collins: "Twitter, because it's fast and easy. I can even schedule through Hootsuite without impacting reach, and does seem to increase my website clicks if I'm pointing people at something specific like a #SampleSunday blog post."

Kim Boykin: "Facebook. I feel more engaged with readers."

Terri Anne Stanley: "I like Twitter for networking with other authors, but Facebook for connecting with potential readers."

Caryl McAdoo: "I prefer Facebook because it's easy to use and I can copy and paste to interested groups or post photos at will."

Sonya Weiss: "I prefer Twitter because it's not as easy to get caught up and waste time as it is on other social media sites. Plus, because people are busy, it's easier for them to take the time to read 140 characters than anything longer."

Anna James: "Facebook because I can link it to my Twitter account and I only have to post in one place."

Kourtney Heintz: "Facebook because it feels natural and is easy to use."

Ashlyn Chase: "Facebook is fun, and I talk about all kinds of things there. I feel I get to know others in a fun way, sharing jokes or pictures. I use Twitter for shout-outs—if a friend asks me to announce her new release, for instance."

Patty Blount: "I'm really enjoying Wattpad for a great network to connect to teens (my target audience). Twitter is great for other writers, but I often feel left out. Facebook is great. Goodreads, I avoid like it has cooties."

Jeannie Moon: "Facebook—it is more interactive for readers and authors."

Jennifer Beckstrand: "I love Facebook because I feel like I can really connect with my readers in a more conversational forum."

Gail Chianese: "I'm on several different social media outlets, but I prefer Facebook over the others. Not that it doesn't have its quirks, but it allows me to interact with others and I have a better chance of seeing all of my friends' comments for the day."

Mary Ellis: "I prefer Facebook for my social interaction since I'm far too long-winded for 140 characters."

Lisa Brown Roberts: "I love Twitter because I think of it as the introverts' cocktail party. If no one laughs at my jokes, I can skitter away and refill my drink without being too embarrassed."

Adrienne Giordano: "I prefer Facebook because I'm not limited to a certain length for my posts and can get creative."

Tawny Weber: "I often think of Twitter as the social media platform for extroverts and Facebook for introverts, which means I'm on Facebook a lot more."

Jen J. Danna: "I love Twitter's brevity—if you can't say it in 140 characters, don't say it at all."

Social media platforms are great tools for audience engagement as long as you commit to participating frequently and perform well. If you find social media intimidating, choose one platform to master. From there, you will build the confidence needed to try another.

However, some social networking sites lend themselves more toward purchases than others. Former Market or Die Author Services, LLC marketer Brian Schmalberger provided the following article for this book. The article, sent to subscribers via the company's newsletter, was compiled using data from Shopify.com and Google DoublClick Ad planner; buying information references consumer buying, yet the findings were interpreted on how the results may be useful for authors. In, *Like It, Tweet It, Pin It*, Schmalberger writes,

"Social media is no longer just for fun. It is a vital component of marketing for authors and businesses alike. What began as a way for friends and family to more easily connect and share has morphed into a means for businesses to target specific audiences. But with so many different social networks available, currently numbering in the hundreds, how do you know which one is best for you? How do you know what network is worth putting your time, energy, and money into? Social media has made advertising and branding accessible to every individual on the web.

"I'll focus on the big three for this article: Facebook, Twitter, and Pinterest. These sites are veritable Goliaths, each vying for your eyes and mouse clicks.

"**Facebook** allows an author or business to create a fan page, curated with different types of media: pictures, videos, and written posts. Fans can 'Like,' comment on, or share postings. Fan pages should be designed to be representative of the brand or product. For authors, this is a great place to share book information and events. Facebook also lends itself well to interacting with fans. Audience 60% female, 40% male.

"**Twitter** is a constantly updated stream of 'tweets,' and each tweet is 140 characters in length. (This may sound odd, but Twitter was founded when text messages were limited to 140 characters.) Tweets can be news headlines, links to external sites, thoughts, and opinions. Twitter is useful to send quick updates to fans, such as a recent book review or release. Audience 60% female, 40% male.

"**Pinterest** is a visual site where images are 'Pinned' to 'Boards.' These collections can be anything: 'Christmas List,' 'Cars,' 'Cute Dogs,' etc.

For authors, Boards can be created for characters, settings, and plots. It is an interesting way to visually give your fans an inside look into how your book was created. Audience 80% female, 20% male.

"The average age across all social media networks is 36.9 years. It is interesting to note that Pinterest leads the 25-34 age bracket and Facebook leads the 45-54 age bracket.

"You spent how much?"

"The average order from Pinterest is nearly $80. This is twice that of Facebook (~$40) and Twitter (~$30). Further, recent reports suggest that buyers referred to sites from Pinterest are 10% more likely to buy an item.

"While there is no one social network that will work for every author, there are different sites for different audiences. Knowing the demographics and behavior of the different networks is powerful marketing information. Combining this information with your genre and target audience, your precious time, energy, and money can be more effectively used.

"The social media universe is a big place. Creating a profile is just the first step in developing an effective web presence. For those who have already taken the plunge and are using social media to reach out to fans, it's important to become more efficient in your postings to make sure you're reaching your target audience. (All statistics reported by Google DoubleClick Ad Planner. Pinterest stats reported by Shopify.)"

Book blogger Sarah Wendell is often asked to give her advice on social media. With almost thirty thousand Twitter followers, she knows how to keep an audience engaged. For this book, Ms. Wendell was asked to provide tips for engaging in social media. She says, "My advice for social media interaction is always these three points:

"1. Develop a social media policy for yourself. Preferably when you're offline. You can look at various corporate social media policies to see how and where large and small companies define their boundaries for employees representing their firms. You can also think about what you like and dislike about other people's social media presences, and how their interactions have made you feel, both positive and negative.

"Once you've developed your policy, hang a copy where you can see it when you're on your computer. If you get pissed off or have a bad moment, you can remind your future self of your boundaries.

"2. Be a person. Despite my suggestion that you look at corporate policies for examples, you're a person. You're not a billboard. Social media is about conversation and interaction, not broadcast. It's okay to incorporate some of the things you're passionate about in what you share online. The things you're passionate about are often what make you most interesting.

"3. Don't be afraid to mess up, and apologize when you do. You will screw up. It's unavoidable. You're human. When you make a mistake, apologize sincerely."

Key takeaways from this chapter:

* If you're not involved in social media, you are missing an opportunity.

* Pros and cons exist for every social media platform. There is no one correct selection. You should choose the platform you are most comfortable with. For beginners, select one platform to master before beginning another.

* Consider joining forces with a fellow author to manage a social media presence in order to combat feelings of being overwhelmed.

Chapter Twelve

What Authors Can Learn from the Business World

People buy books in order to feel good, to be transported into another world, or for education. Yet, with so many books promising to deliver these experiences, it becomes difficult for an author to stand out.

Living the life of a full-time author can feel a bit like Rapunzel locked away in a tower, only, instead of releasing hair, authors release books into the world. And, because writing is a solitary profession, you can miss out on lessons learned by corporate America that can be applied to your career.

Earlier, this book talked about brand as a way for authors to stand out in a crowd. But there is a difference between standing out and catapulting your brand to the top. Like corporate America, you can take brand one step further. No longer is the brand belief "if you build it, they will come." With the revenue many corporations are expected to generate, they do not have the time to take a passive approach to their brand management, nor should you. Instead, they have created and measured themselves in what is known as mindshare.

According to BusinessDictionary.com, mindshare is, "Informal measure of the amount of talk, mention, or reference an idea, firm or product generates in the public or media."

Mindshare takes up space in the mind of the consumer. Building mind-share focuses on the quantity and frequency that a consumer thinks about a brand. Throughout this book, brand is mentioned as an integral piece to your marketing. You need a brand to build mindshare. To build mindshare, you, through your books and marketing, have to become memorable. Mindshare means that if a reader is thinking about an author, the reader will buy that particular author, and buy them repeatedly.

Mindshare lends itself to market share. The more you are thought about, the more you are bought. The more you are bought, the greater the sales, and the greater you become in the industry. So how do you begin to create mindshare? The steps are simple.

* Offer a good quality product (novel, novella, short story, etc.).
* Build a brand.
* Make the product available for purchase everywhere.
* Market and build audience engagement.
* Repeat.

Sound easy? Good. It is. Any mass-marketed product has to build and maintain mindshare. Why? Because with mass-marketed products, the competition is tremendous. Think about everyday items, such as soap, paper towels, or candy bars. For the most part, these products change very little, if at all. And, if a product doesn't change, why should a consumer care about it?

Therefore, getting a consumer not only to remember a specific brand of soap, but also purchase the brand is a big, big win. And, isn't that what you are trying to achieve? For readers not only to remember you, but buy your books, too?

Let's take a moment and explore how corporate America builds mindshare.

Again, the theory is simple to understand. Businesses assign personalities to their brand, and change them routinely to suit their marketing needs. Savvy marketing executives apply the research of Carl Jung's twelve archetypes and assign a personality archetype to corporate entities with the hopes of bringing business and consumer closer together.

Authors who wish to read about Jung's research can do so by logging on to: psychology.about.com/od/personalitydevelopment/tp/archetypes.htm

And if corporate America can do it, you certainly can.

First, it is important to examine how mindshare is built. For you to create mindshare, you should determine the mindshare you wish to own. That is to say, you must decide and commit to how you want people to talk about your brand.

What personality do you want to bestow on your brand?

How do you wish to be perceived long-term?

Do you wish to be known as humorous, sexy, witty, dark, or intellectual? Decide what the nature of your brand is. Here are some suggestions:

* Innocent/Sweet. Characteristics: idealistic, optimistic, hopeful.

Author example: Debbie Macomber

* Dark. Characteristics: thought-provoking, disturbing, intense.

Author example: Stephen King

* Sexy. Characteristics: passionate, seductive, alluring.

Author example: E.L. James

* Intellectual. Characteristics: educated, thought leader, maven.

Author example: Malcom Gladwell

* Savior. Characteristics: strong against adversity, heroic, forceful.

Author example: Tom Clancy

* Magical. Characteristics: creator of new worlds, dreamy, fantastical.

Author example: George R.R. Martin

* Witty. Characteristics: absurdity, sarcastic, tongue-in-cheek.

Author example: Max Brooks

* Adventurer. Characteristics: quest-oriented, problem-solving, inquisitive.

Author example: Dan Brown

Once you decide on your brand's personality, it is imperative that you commit to it. Why? Because this personality will be associated with the brand, and just as you want to eliminate brand confusion, you don't want your target audience to become unable to describe the characteristics of your preferred brand.

You should find comfort in knowing there are ways to build mindshare and make your brand memorable. You must communicate your brand characteristics to your audience. Learning how to do this is as easy as watching one hour of television commercials with a critical eye. Think for a moment about a favorite television commercial. What makes it so memorable? What likable qualities does it include? Jot down the answers. Spending time dissecting television commercials for mass-marketed products will teach you valuable lessons about mindshare.

Very artfully and quite subliminally, corporate America feeds consumers beliefs about a product. They repeatedly tell the buying public how much they should care and why. It isn't uncommon to see commercials drone on about the strength of a wet paper towel, or what might happen should drivers succumb to the pitfalls of cut-rate car insurance. It may sound like a gimmick. It's not. It is a tactic used to build mindshare.

When you think about building mindshare, it is important that you can articulate how you would like to be remembered. And, how you would like the reader to remember you must tie in with your brand. What emotion do you want the reader to feel when discussing your work with a friend?

Corporations communicate such messages, and so should you.

Here are a few examples of commercials to watch on YouTube which are a good sampling of building mindshare in the mind of the buying public. Remember, mindshare combines message with emotion.

Want to be known as emotional? Search online for these commercials:
 * "Dear Sophie" from Google
 * "Christmas Commercial 2013" from Publix
 * "Puppy Love" from Budweiser

Want to be known as humorous? Search online for these commercials:
 * "Betty White" by Snickers
 * "Hump Day" by Geico
 * "Time Out with Dog" by E*TRADE

Want to be known as absurd? Search online for these commercials:
* "Farting Horse" by Budweiser
* "Doritos Ostrich" by Frito-Lay
* "A Conference Call in Real Life" by Tripp and Tyler

Or do you want to promote value? In every Geico commercial, the company promotes the value of their brand. The message "Fifteen minutes could save fifteen percent or more on car insurance," is more than a slogan. Their tagline is what they want the consumer to know most about their mass-marketed product. They compete on price.

Once you can boil down what it is you want their readership to know most about your brand, you can begin building mindshare.

Authors are creative people. It's logical that they would be eager to take the next step in brand evolution—building mindshare. The commercials mentioned above include stories, music, and images to appeal to the heartstrings, funny bone, or educational interests of the consumer. Could you not do the same via a book trailer?

Take a moment and think about a recently viewed book trailer. Name something the author could have done differently to make the video more compelling.

What you should glean through these video examples is that when emotion is tied to messaging, the combination makes the brand memorable, builds mindshare, gets people talking, and sets the stage for repeat purchases.

I encourage you to put emotion into all of the marketing materials you create. Brand statements, story taglines, social media messages, printed materials, and videos should use images and text together to convey the emotion behind the brand needed to create mindshare.

Iconic Brands

There are many different choices of chocolate bars on the market, but there's only one Hershey's. There are millions of romance novels available for sale, yet there's only one Nora Roberts. So, if all that is needed is to tie emotion to a message to stand out in a crowd, why do some brands never reach "iconic" status? Iconic brands are distinctive, have favorable associations, and maintain a core fan base with a strong emotional connection to the author. There are a few key elements which can hinder you from reaching your full potential as a brand icon. They are:

> * Inconsistency. With many paths now available to authors for publication, you may be enticed to stretch yourself beyond the limits of your brand. Temptations may become too great to "try new things," so that you become distracted from your core focus. The romance writer who chooses to write fantasy may find it's difficult for her audience to cross over. Therefore, she will have to start fresh with marketing herself.
> * Confusion. The inability to distill your brand down to a few characteristics can confuse the consumer when making a buying decision.
> * Poor Product Quality. Stories that are published that are of lesser quality than what the audience has become accustomed to can damage your potential.
> * Change in Consumer Preferences. Probably most heartbreaking is if you have produced consistent, quality books, but the tastes of the market change. In this instance, you are helpless and have no other choice but to "stay the course" until the market moves back in your favor. However, the temptation to follow trends may become too great to ignore.

Brand Rejuvenation

Even established iconic brands face storms. Crisis happens in business routinely and these crises affect how much of the consumer's mindshare the brand retains. Case in point: over the 2013 holiday shopping season, retail giant Target suffered a data security breach, leaving many customers wondering if their private information had fallen into the wrong hands.   This crisis came at an unfortunate time for the company who was already losing ground.

The company's handling of the situation was criticized by consumers and the media despite Target's notification to customers that they were addressing the issue in the media, on their website, and via direct mail. The *Los Angeles Daily News* reported, "angry Target customers expressed their frustration on the company's Facebook page." (A. D'Innocenzio, December 20, 2013, "Target customers angered over response to credit card data breach." *Los Angeles Daily News*, Retrieved from dailynews.com)

The situation did not bode well for the retail giant. Falling victim to such a crisis during a peak shopping season hurt their marketing efforts. The article by *The Los Angeles Daily News* went on to say, "The incident is particularly troublesome for Target because it has used its store-branded credit and debit cards as a marketing tool to attract shoppers with a five percent discount."

Clearly, the retailer's problem was twofold. In order to win back customers, Target needed to not only repair, but improve their security measures to demonstrate they could be responsible with consumer data and bring their customers back the feeling of safety they'd once had. Secondly, the store needed to create a reason for their customers to return. Simply fixing a security issue wasn't going to be enough. Why? They'd lost mindshare. Too much competition exists which makes customers more likely to go elsewhere, someplace they can get similar products for the same, or cheaper prices.

The lesson here for you is that, even after you establish a brand, maybe one even considered iconic, you need to continually work to ensure consumer loyalty. You may never have to worry about security breaches on the scale of Target, but that is not the point. The point is, if the brand does not consistently provide what the consumer is accustomed to buying, consumers will go elsewhere. Brands cannot afford to rest on their laurels because, if left unmaintained, consumer mindshare will deteriorate.

The shakiness left under the consumers' feet after the Target crisis is slow to stabilize.

Nearly five months after the disaster, *USA Today* reported, "As competitors like Walmart offer better prices and others like Macy's and Amazon offer better digital experiences, Target has lost its 'Tar-jay' cachet. 'The insides of competing stores are rapidly changing' Sozzi says, 'and there is Target, still trying to live off of a cheap chic reputation it hasn't earned for three years.'" (H. Malcom, May 21, 2013, "Target has lost its cheap, chic edge," *USA Today*, Retrieved from usatoday.com/story/money/business/2014/05/21/target-refocus-priorities/9376403/)

You would be mistaken in believing day-to-day business dealings cannot provide valuable lessons to the writing community. You are essentially your own small business. And you do need to understand what you can control when industry dealings trickle down and affect you. Here, I am specifically speaking about the very public disagreement between Amazon and Hachette Book Group. In summary, Amazon and Hachette Book Group allowed the public into their behind-closed-door discussions regarding e-book pricing, and other topics to which they cannot agree. This "feud" affected the ability of titles to be pre-ordered, shipped on time, and didn't allow books to be made available for purchase as consumers have become accustomed to on Amazon.

Authors had no control over the outcome of the negotiations, but this conflict has provided a great lesson for authors regarding the importance of mindshare. If you have worked diligently to build the necessary mindshare, it will pull the reader toward your inner circle. The reader will be more likely to purchase your book from any available venue. The goal of mindshare is to keep the reader's mind on you, or the books themselves.

True fans and buyers will find the desired product, even if it means a disruption in their usual buying pattern. Do conflicts like the Amazon/Hachette disagreement damage discoverability? Yes. But, to combat the discoverability issue, the theory stands that if you widen the inner circle, the outer circle will grow as well, lending itself to bigger and bigger mindshare.

Key points to keep in mind when building mindshare are:
   * Focus on outreach. Try new ideas with the sole purpose of growing your inner circle. Take risks.
   * Brainstorm ways to keep your brand known.
   * Use multiple communication mediums. Mix it up. Do not rely solely on social media.
   * Always produce quality products.
   * Take time to review past efforts and plan for the future.
   * Strengthen relationships with readers, editors, agents, publicists, fellow authors, and other industry professionals.

If you keep a keen eye on corporate America, there are multiple lessons you can learn, teaching that will provide value. From learning how to create mindshare, learning the value of being able to assign a personality to a brand, and create "buzz," corporate America can be a valuable teacher. Industries repeatedly communicate why consumers should prefer their brand over another, and when done tactfully, you should do the same because it is the key to making you memorable. However, the best key to becoming memorable is through the story itself, which is your sole responsibility.

Key takeaways from this chapter:

* Mindshare is an informal measure of the amount of talk, mention, or reference a product generates in the marketplace.

* Building mindshare focuses on the quantity and frequency that consumers think about a brand.

* You need a brand to build mindshare.

* Businesses assign personalities to their brand and change them to suit their marketing needs.

* Iconic brands are distinctive, have favorable associations, and maintain a core fan base with strong emotional ties to the author.

* Even after brands are established, they need to work continually to ensure consumer loyalty.

* Brands cannot afford to rest on their laurels because mindshare will deteriorate.

* Authors are their own small businesses.

Chapter Thirteen

Measuring the Sustainable Plan

Too many authors make yes or no decisions with regard to their market-ing based on the results of one promotion. This activity can be detri-mental to a career. Why? Without understanding what you should meas-ure, how to measure result activity, and how to interpret results, you may react too soon and disregard essential activities without understanding the full impact of your promotions on your marketing plan as a whole.

Here, you should not build a plan to obtain the data, but learn how to interpret it to achieve your best results. The focus of this chapter will be to determine what to measure, how to measure, and, where applicable, provide benchmarks to decide if results were, indeed, successful.

Effective Communications

In Chapter One, you learned how to write effective communication. Effectiveness of communication is easily measured in social media. Look for the number of likes, shares, and comments or retweets to particular posts. Has the engagement improved over previous posts? Is the audience responding more or less than prior to changing up the communication?

Results of this kind of measurement are not statistically significant, be-cause with some social media platforms, all posts are not viewed by all fans/followers/friends at the same time. However, with more effective communication, you should notice an increase in sales volume and readership. If you do not, or if the sales volume or readership numbers have dropped, ensure links are provided on all communication, the call to action is clear, and the messaging is properly layered. And lastly, ensure you don't use any hard-sell messages.

Target Audience

The first and most crucial metric for you to measure is your target audience. Ask yourself if your fans and followers meet the targets built in the profile. Compile a brief survey and distribute it to the readership via your newsletter, website, and social media platforms. Use the results to gauge how well you performed against the predicted targets. While the survey results will not be statistically significant, you can use them as an indication for how well you performed against your predictions.

In the survey, I recommend you ask the readership how they learned about you. Make sure all of your communication efforts are listed. Did the reader discover your website? Follow you on social media? Discover you via an event or conference? If so, which one? Or, were you discovered while browsing in a bookstore?

It is common to ask for age by providing age ranges. The most common age ranges are thirteen to seventeen, eighteen to twenty-four, twenty-five to thirty-four, thirty-five to forty-four, forty-five to fifty-four, fifty-five to sixty-four, and sixty-five years and older. Ask them for their gender.

If possible, ask them to list what authors besides you they like to read. Answers to this question can become helpful when compiling an author landscape analysis. Be sure to ask them where they shop for books. Ask which websites and stores they visit. This information can help you determine where to advertise. Ask the reader about any other hobbies or interests they have. Look for commonalities.

Results from a reader survey can not only help you determine if you attracted your target audience, but if you did not, it will assist you in making adjustments to your marketing plan. For example, if the population of the readership aged younger (or older) than expected, you may be required to make a decision about which social media outlets you should utilize in order to engage with a different audience.

Repeat the survey periodically. This will allow you to make updates and changes necessary to expand your reach.

Digital Advertising

When placing an order for digital advertising, you should not be intimidated to ask the blog, website, or magazine, how and when the metrics will be communicated. After all, the decision to place a digital ad on a particular blog, site, or magazine may have come from a referral from a fellow author, a publicist, or the author's own research instead of being sold to you via a media sales representative.

Terms you should become familiar with in response to measuring digital activity are the following:

* Impression. Number of impressions basically refers to the number of times your ad was displayed.

* Clicks. The number of times a viewer clicked on your ad.

* Click-Through Rate (CTR). The number of times a viewer went to a hyperlink as a result of clicking the ad, generally reported as a percentage. This percentage refers to the number of clicks an ad received, dividing it by the number of impressions, and then multiplying by 100.

* Cost Per Click (CPC). The amount of money owed for each click.

* Conversion Rate (CVR). The number of clicks on the ad that gets the viewer to perform a certain action (filling out a form, making a purchase, registering for the newsletter, etc.). It is calculated by taking the number of conversions an ad received, dividing by the number of clicks, then multiplying by 100.

* Cost Per Action. The amount of money owed for each action taken by the viewer (making a purchase, filling out a form, etc.).

When evaluating digital advertising results, keep in mind bigger is better. You want to look for a large number of impressions, clicks, click-throughs, and, where applicable, conversions. As mentioned in previous chapters, a major obstacle in digital advertising is lack of budget. Not only is it costly to place the ad, but then you must fund any costs for the ad to be created. Price ranges for digital ads can range from the hundreds, to the thousands, to the hundreds of thousands for high traffic websites like *People Magazine*. Therefore, you should place your dollars where you can get the most impressions from your target audience for the least amount of investment.

Also, it is important to advertise digitally on the same site three times before making a determination if the site is worth a continued investment. Chart your results and measure increases. For best results, place the ad on or near the banner. Banner ads are generally the most expensive. This is because research has proven that website viewers read in a Z-like pattern. Therefore, when choosing ad positioning, if the top banner is not available, secure the next position in the Z for greater visibility.

Print Advertising

Like digital advertising, you should evaluate print advertising by number of impressions. However, make sure you are interpreting the number of impressions correctly. Look at their advertising impressions. This is the number of people who will be exposed to the ad. Media (or print) impressions are the number of copies produced/sold. For ad impressions, it's not unusual for the numbers to be extremely high. That is because it is not calculated in a 1:1 ratio. One magazine sold does not equal one ad view. Extra views are built into the calculation to allow for additional non-purchased views (for example, the magazine at the doctor's office waiting room that is viewed by many).

Impressions are not the only measure of print advertising. Another metric you want to note is pre-and post-advertising web traffic. Note the number of visitors to your site before running the ad, measure it during the weeks the ad runs, and continue to measure after the ad is removed from circulation. Ideally, you would like to see a spike in website traffic.

Also, you should measure activity pre-and post-ad run. Be sure to note any uptick in newsletter subscriptions, emails received, or increases in social media fans and followers.

Lastly, redemption rates can be used in measuring print advertising. Should the ad contain a coupon or promo code, the redemption of these can be used to track success of an ad placement. Ensure the coupon or promo code is specific to the newspaper or magazine if you are running multiple ads. This way you can track which outlets outperformed the others.

Again, with print advertising, it is imperative to make the call to action clear to the reader. If you are measuring the ad on redemption rates, the reader must know what action needs to be performed as a result of the ad.

Newsletter

Many online newsletter platforms include measurement and analysis as part of their services, which is a good time savings for authors. Sites often display charts showing how the author fares compared to a previous mailing, but what they may fail to do is give the information to know if they are performing well or poorly. For newsletter metrics, it is important to pay attention to the open rate.

Open rate is generally displayed as a percentage and it represents the percent of newsletter subscribers who opened the newsletter. A benchmark for an open rate of a well-performing newsletter is twenty-five to thirty percent.

If your open rate is less than twenty-five to thirty percent, take steps in order to improve the open rate. A very simple step in improving the number is to avoid the spam filter. Verify that the newsletter does not contain sentences in all CAPS, and avoid the use of unnecessary exclamation points; both of these can increase the potential of the newsletter being marked as spam.

Secondly, the subject line for the newsletter is very important. Make sure to keep the subject descriptor simple. Plain descriptions such as, "June's news from Tawny Weber," or "Your Market or Die Newsletter is here," help your newsletter avoid the spam filter, plus simple descriptions let the reader know what they have received without telling them what's inside.

Think about it. If you tell the reader MY BOOK RELEASES JUNE 2 in the subject line, what need does the reader have to open the newsletter? So, he or she doesn't, and, by default, misses out on other valuable information.

Like digital advertising, the click-through rate is also important to newsletters. An acceptable click-through rate should range from three to four percent. If you are looking to increase your click-through rate, remember the Z-like pattern discussed in digital advertising. If you choose to use a book cover and link in your newsletter, like in advertising, place the cover and purchase link near the top of the newsletter communication to help increase the click-through rate.

Another metric to track is number of subscribers. Chart the number to ensure the number of subscribers is always increasing, while aiming to keep the number of unsubscribes to less than 1%. You should communicate the existence of your newsletter, and where it is located, in all reader-facing promotional activity.

Blogs

Bloggers are busy and influential people, and while it is not always possible to get reported metrics for every stop on a blog tour, if you can solicit information from the blogger, especially the ones who manage blogs less than a year old, about the metrics of their site, it is good to ask for the following:

> * Number of subscribers. Subscribers are people who sign up to receive information/articles from the blog. Generally, an email is sent from the blog to every subscriber with every new post. Many blogs also take into account their social media fans and followers as subscribers since some blogging sites skew reporting metrics.

> * Number of comments. Number of comments reveals how engaged the audience is with the blog itself. You should evaluate the blog and read comments left by the readers. Judge the level of engagement and tailor your post to the personality of the blog to maximize the number of comments.

> * Number of site/blog hits. This is a tricky metric because a blog can continue to receive hits (visits) days, weeks, or months after your post goes live. Some blogs post the number of hits they've received on their site. Others choose to keep their numbers close to the vest.

You can also take part in the measure of your own success and failure on a blog tour. Success can be measured in the number of hits back on your own blog or website, the number of engaging comments, and by simply booking yourself on popular well-known blogs. Research the blogs in your genre and become aware of the big ones that everyone reads.

Measures of failure may be if you failed to participate in responding to comments, if you did not provide a link to your own website, or if you didn't research properly and built a blog tour made of blogs no one cares to read.

Contests

Contests need to be measured based on the goal of the contest. If the goal of the contest is to build your brand via newsletter subscriptions, then you would measure the number of subscribers during the span of the contest. If the goal of the contest is to increase sales, then the number of sales should be analyzed pre-and post-contest duration.

With any contest, measuring simply on participation rates may not be the most accurate form of measurement, especially when the prize is free books. There will be many who enter a contest simply to see if they win, but never intend to purchase the book. Therefore, contests which are created to perform an action, besides simply entering, lend themselves toward building a more engaged readership.

Reviews

Today, reviews can be found for nearly everything, such as restaurants, hotel rooms, or any product which can be sold online. Reviews help consumers decide what product is right for them. Reviews can also help a book stand out in the marketplace. On certain sites, like Amazon, the number and quality of reviews act as influencers to the buying public. Reviews, consumer or professional, can help a book generate the needed buzz to sustain its salability. Book review sites and magazines are equally important to a book's ability to generate word-of-mouth buzz and sales success. Since you should not have an influence over the quality of the review (i.e., paying for positive reviews), you should focus and measure yourself on the number of reviews received.

Focus on your communication to the readership. Tell readers about the importance reviews have to a book's longevity in the marketplace. With this understanding, the general public may be more apt to not only read the book, but review the work as well.

About a year ago, buzz in the industry spread that approximately thirty reviews on book-buying sites sent a title into automatic promotion. However, this is no longer the case. You should focus on varied reviews. Should a book receive all five-star reviews, the buyer may feel wary that the reviews have been manipulated. You should prepare yourself to take the good reviews with the bad, because a mix of honest reviews lends credibility to the book, and its author.

Press

Attracting the attention of the press is one of the more difficult ways to obtain buzz for a book. Reporters are busy, always on a deadline, and need to be impressed in order to cover a book or its author. Reporters have a responsibility to deliver quality material to their audience. The media expects to be pitched. Therefore, any amount of free press you obtain, whether it is a newspaper article, television appearance, online press release distribution, radio mention, or interview, is a win.

Don't pitch the media directly. The use of an in-house or freelance publicist often brings quicker results because of their personal connections with media professionals. Do consider every media opportunity a publicist brings to you as a huge win, big or small in number and audience. Know the publicist's efforts were more than sending an email and scheduling an interview. Like authors, queries from publicists are often declined.

However, if you don't have an in-house publicist or the resources to hire a publicist to work the media, you can make connections in the media by properly researching local reporters who cover books. Read the reporters' columns and respond to them. Building a connection helps the reporter learn your name, so that when you send a request for interview, your name will not be foreign.

Conventions and Events

Measuring success at conventions and events should be measured in quantity. Since one of the goals for these events should be to get the author's name "out there," measure success in quantifiable tasks. For example, during a book signing, how many readers did you meet? How many books did you sign or sell? How many business cards did you give away? How many promotional items did you give away? How many readers subscribed to your newsletter? If you spoke at the event or taught a workshop, how many people attended? How many people did you recruit to your street team/fan club?

You should have a goal for each convention or event you attend. Without quantifiable measurement, you may feel that you have wasted your time and money, and be unable to determine if your participation in an event was successful.

Also note, it make take more than one time participating in an event to know if a particular convention is a good place to invest. If you don't have the time or money to attend the event as a participant before joining in as an author, you should pulse your network for anecdotal feedback. However, judge the feedback with an open mind. Ask for quantifiable numbers.

Before attending a convention or event, it is important to perform the proper research on the venue, the event company, if applicable, and, if possible, look for the past number of attendees. You may also want to search online for any/all promotional activity performed by the convention/event to attract attendees. Some events do an exceptional job of attracting authors, but fall flat in their efforts to attract actual readers. I encourage you to conduct proper research prior to the event.

Direct Mail

A direct mail campaign is performed when a piece of marketing material is mailed to a physical address. Should you choose a direct mail campaign, a general rule of thumb is to expect a response rate of no more than one to three percent. A major exception to this percentage is if you are mailing to a list of proven contacts that have provided their address and requested the mailing. Direct mail marketing tends not to work well on overly complex marketing campaigns. The easiest type of direct mail campaign for an author to execute is for the piece to contain a coupon or promotion code that can be redeemed by the reader.

However, direct mail can be effective if you use it in conjunction (or as a communication tool to enhance) a bigger promotional effort. For example, if you are selling books with a discounted price on a particular website, you may push the responders via the direct mail piece to a specific landing page. The mailing may have no impact on how many people respond, but it may assist in converting a reader from browser to buyer.

Measuring success for a direct mail campaign is as simple as tracking the action requested by the communication, i.e., responses, website hits. Allow for a longer duration of time in tracking for any issues that may arise in the postal process.

Website

It is not uncommon for an author or their website personnel to install some type of analytical measurement coding into their website, check the stats occasionally, and move on. Should you wish to improve the performance of your site, I recommend a trifecta approach when measuring success. Yes, gross analytics are important, but equally essential are engagement and conversion metrics.

Therefore, begin a spreadsheet for your website analytics which includes standard metrics such as:

* Time spent on the website. This will tell you how engaging, entertaining, or informative the website is.

* Number of unique visitors. Unique visitors are website visitors who only visit the site once. If a person visits a site on Thursday, then again on Friday, the action is recorded as two visits from one visitor (generally tracked by the visitor's unique IP address).

* Number of pages viewed per visit. This metric determines how many pages the visitor viewed during each visit.

* Most viewed page. Allows you to know what page on the site is viewed the most by visitors.

* New vs. returning visitors. Measured by the unique IP addresses of visitors.

* Total number of hits. The retrieval of an item from a web server.

* Hits by country. The retrieval of an item from a web server by country location.

* Number of downloads (if applicable). Copying of data from one source to another.

Other formats the author should examine are:

* Traffic sources. You should be aware of the drivers who lead traffic to your site (paid vs. organic searches, keywords, direct traffic, referrals, links, etc.).

* Flow visualization. Allows you to see the path the reader takes when they visit the site. It provides answers to how the visitor navigates the site.

There are many tools available to an author for measuring website traffic. I and my publisher do not endorse any of the sites listed, but have made a selection available for you to investigate on your own. They are: Google Analytics, Google Website Optimizer, Stat Counter, Piwik, AW Stats, and Analog.

All of these metrics are good to know and important to monitor. Track monthly and record all findings. However, your analysis should not stop at website traffic metrics alone. Conversion is also an important metric. Again, conversion means the attempt to turn someone who is "just browsing" into an "engaged book-buying reader." For conversion, you must ensure the website contains the pathways needed for the reader to complete an action. The goal is to bring someone who is looking at the site into the fold and convert them from the outer circle to your inner circle. To do this, you should ensure you have provided the following tools:

* Purchase links or buttons for every outlet where the books are sold online.

* List of information/retailers for where the books are sold in stores.

* Information on where to find you in social media.

* Easy to find and hassle-free newsletter registrations.

* Your contact information or email address.

* Other relevant information such as your agent's information or how to obtain film rights.

Your traffic and conversion numbers are only going to be successful if you have built a proper engagement strategy into the site. Think of the engagement portion of the website as adding in the "human element" to the page. The goal here is to show the reader that you are more than someone who writes books. Evaluate the site's personality and check for the following:

* The site is communicating your brand message and conveys emotion.

* The site contains a photo of the author.

* The site offers a few personal details about the author.

* The site lists any/all organizations or charities supported by the author.

* Blurbs or excerpts are listed for all books.

By evaluating a website's activity as a whole, you can gauge where adjustments need to be made in order to improve the site's overall performance. When making changes, it's important to make them in small numbers and track the results; that way you will know what levers to move to stimulate activity going forward.

Street Teams/Fan Clubs

If you have made a commitment to build a street team or fan club, most likely you would like to know if the team is worth its continued investment. There are several ways to measure fan club engagement. Some authors like to measure each member of the team by assigning points to the people, or teams, who perform tasks related to book promotion. These points then build and accumulate which lead to special prizes or gifts awarded by the authors. Authors who measure their teams in this fashion may choose to assign the task to a personal assistant.

Should you not want to encourage competition among super fans, you may want to incorporate task-based rewards via a system of checks and balances. For example, if the goal of the team is to take a trip to their local bookstore with the intent of finding your book and displaying it face-out on the shelf, snapping a photo and posting it to Facebook then tagging the author may be sufficient for you to know team members are doing their "job."

Sometimes, you will wonder how you can manage a non-performing member of a street team and when or if you should ever delete someone from your club. My advice is that you should never directly "oust" someone from your fan club unless that person has made a negative impact on your brand. To that end, there are a few ways to manage the team to eliminate underperforming members in order to guarantee peak performance:

* Communicate regularly that the team is voluntary. Let the team know that they can opt out at any time without any hard feelings or grievances. Let the team members know that you recognize and respect everyone's free time, so if the member is unable or unwilling to invest the time required for the team, dropping out is okay.

* Communicate to the team that you will be reorganizing your team database. Therefore, anyone who does not confirm their willingness and participation to the team within a certain period of time could be deleted.

* Consciously leave out members from mailings, etc. who do not participate to evaluate their response.

* Personally email the member and inquire of their participation. Be sure to ask if they are okay and if there is anything you can do to help.

Social Media

Many social media platforms, like Facebook, Twitter, and Pinterest, have associated analytical measurement systems which are advantageous for authors to learn and use. However, some platforms routinely change the algorithms behind the way posts are viewed, therefore enticing the author to pay for wide-reaching distribution of their messages. In this section, you will learn how to measure your social media performance by knowing terminology, evaluating performance, and becoming familiar with measurement tools to increase social media engagement.

Facebook

Facebook's fan pages are chock-full of valuable measurement information. Because Facebook readily changes the workings of their platform without prior notice, should you require step-by-step instructions on how to obtain analytical information in detail, please consult the Facebook Help Center located on facebook.com.

Your fan page will offer a quick summary of the week's activity. Facebook will list the number of page likes and post reach. Page likes refers to the number of new fans who have clicked "like" on the page. Post reach is the number of people who have viewed the page. Notification is the number of activities (likes, comments, shares) which have occurred on your page. Messages refer to the number of direct messages a page receives.

To view demographic data for people who like your fan page, click "Insights" on your author page, then click "People." In the "Your Fans" section, you will be able to see the percentage of people who liked the page, the gender breakdown, country and city information, and preferred language.

To view information regarding what day of the week your fans are online and the time of day they are most active, click on the "Insights" page, then click "Posts." According to Facebook, data is shown in a one-week period, and the time is set to the local time according to the user's computer. Try to time postings around the time your audience is most active.

To analyze the number of likes the page receives, click "Insights," then click "Likes." There, you can view total page likes, like by date, and where likes came from. You are encouraged to monitor this page in accordance with the different promotional activities you perform on Facebook. Track the activity to the number of likes received.

Knowing where to find analytical information on Facebook is important, but understanding how to interpret the data is even more valuable. For example, you should examine how well your posts are performing by clicking on "Insights," then "Posts." From there, select posts which have performed well. These posts will have the largest reach. Look at the bigger numbers. Here, it is important to determine what you did right. What did you do within the popular posts to make the audience react? Did you:

* Post a visual or contextual theme?
* Post an image?
* Post a question on a "hot topic"?
* Post a favorite quote from your book?
* Post informational content?
* Include something personal about yourself?
* Ask for feedback?

Understand what you did correctly and continue to provide those types of posts to your audience. The personality of every audience is different. Therefore, what works for one author may not work for another.

Twitter

Here, you will find a discussion of three no-charge platforms which measure Twitter activity and different types of analysis of each. The first is TweetReach, tweetreach.com. This no-cost platform allows you to run reports on your Twitter account name or a hashtag. Since TweetReach is a third-party service, the platform will request access to your Twitter account. Simply run a report and you will be provided a snapshot which tells you the estimated reach of your tweets, the number of impressions, activity, top contributors, and a timeline of Twitter activity.

As with Facebook, over time, you should monitor your Twitter activity to identify posts which perform better than others. Here, you may also learn that a popular post on Facebook may not translate to an equally popular post on Twitter. Why? Because they are two separate audiences with different personalities.

For a quick check of daily performance, I recommend <u>SumAll.com</u>. It is a free tool dedicated to the monitoring of quantitative metrics.

With SumAll, you are provided both daily and weekly performance updates. This platform is a simple listing of the number of mentions, tweets, followers, a count of how many people you are following, mentions, mention reach, retweets, retweet reach, and favorite posts. You should use this tool as a quick reference to determine a rise or fall in activity.

Use caution when evaluating performance and do not make decisions based on quantitative metrics alone. Quantitative metrics have specific numbers related to them, but they cannot show you how a message is perceived by an audience.

Therefore, I also encourage you to survey your readership for qualitative metrics when you need more than numbers-oriented feedback.

To determine what time of day to tweet or learn valuable information about followers or people the author follows, Followerwonk is a free site which allows for more demographic-based Twitter activity (<u>followerwonk.com</u>). At the time of writing this book, this free site allows you to view a listing of followers' locations, gender, activity by time zone, etc. It also allows you to compare yourself to other Twitter users, which may uncover interesting data to be included in a future author landscape analysis.

Combining the three platforms and analyzing the data of each, while time-consuming, can lead you to make your most informed decisions in regard to optimizing your Twitter performance.

Pinterest

Analytics with regard to Pinterest have been slow to take off. However, if you are interested in measuring your Pinterest performance, Tailwind (<u>tailwind.com</u>) provides a free dashboard report. Pay attention to the "Track Growth" section. From there, you can track the performance of your Pinterest account. Under "Your Profile," you can review statistics for how well your pins are performing. You will be able to determine how many pins, repins, and likes a board receives.

PinAlerts is a website which will allow you to create a notification when content is pinned from a website.

If you are concerned about growing your Pinterest following, Pinvovle is a website which links Facebook and Pinterest accounts. Syncing accounts can help to grow a fan base.

As with Facebook and Twitter, you should look for successful posts, sometimes noted by the large or frequent number of repins. Determine the attributes that makes the post resonate with the audience, and feed the audience's appetites for this type of communication.

The Importance of Postmortem Analysis

The publishing industry as a whole is a work-forward business. Manuscripts completed and sold today may not be available to readers for months or years. Therefore, it may seem uncommon for you to be asked to stop and examine past activities to predict mistakes from occurring in the future. However, in a Postmortem Analysis (sometimes called a Root Cause Analysis), it is exactly what I'm asking you to do.

Postmortems are easy for companies who manufacture products, but much more difficult for an author who has an emotional investment in his or her work. A postmortem analysis is a process which is conducted at the conclusion of a particular project to determine successes and failures. It is essentially figuring out what worked and what didn't. One advantage of a postmortem analysis is that the process will help identify past mistakes so that you can avoid repeating them. It also serves as confirmation for what you did correctly. One disadvantage is that postmortem analyses take time for data measurement and interpretation. Since authors are always working forward to meet deadlines, the needed time to complete the analysis isn't always readily available. Another disadvantage is that, without outside help, you may be too close to your marketing plan to objectively evaluate it.

Postmortem analysis uses both quantitative and qualitative data. The analysis of both types of results combined helps you to pinpoint what went right vs. what went wrong. The best time to conduct a postmortem analysis is three to six months past the release date. If independently published, you should allow for a minimum of three months of sales data before beginning an analysis.

It is important to write down anything negative which may have affected sales, brand-building, or engagement. And, it is equally important to write down anything positive which impacted sales, brand-building, or engagement efforts. Then, for all positives and negatives, list the causes, then list reasons for the causes. Where applicable, drill down until you can determine why something happened which may have impacted the marketing plan, and then assign corrective actions. Sounds tricky. It's not.

An example is listed below:

* **Positive**: Made Amazon Top 100 list two weeks after release of book.

    * Cause: List all activities which would have had an impact on the result. For example, book was selected as a top pick by XYZ magazine.

    * Reason: Publicist pitched XYZ magazine; secured review June 2014.

* **Positive**: Received nineteen reader reviews on day of release

    * Cause: Successfully communicated the need for honest reviews in social media.

    * Reason: Engaged in social media four or more hours daily post-release.

* **Positive**: Significant sales spike at end of first week.

    * Cause: Released email to newsletter subscribers during first week of release, included buy link.

* **Negative:** No increase in newsletter subscribers for past twelve weeks.

    * Cause: Newsletter registrations were not promoted along with book release.

    * Reason: Discovered registration site not working properly. Sent to webmaster for repair. Estimated repair date July 31.

    * Actions Needed: Test registration site and promote newsletter sign-ups.

* **Negative:** Ten percent drop in the number of retweeted Twitter posts.

    * Cause: While under sales pressure to make a bestseller list, communication messages turned from soft-sell engagement to hard-sell messages which included buy links.

    * Reason: Followers are unlikely to retweet hard-sell messaging.

* Actions Needed: Pre-write future Twitter posts and schedule via Hootsuite to avoid tweets written under pressure.

Continue listing the positive and negative outcomes of the book until the list is exhausted. Where possible, you will want to use detailed, number-driven data. However, it is also important to remember not to become bogged down with data and information which is out of your control. Postmortem analysis should be used as a vehicle which allows you to brainstorm what you could have done differently, so that you are better prepared for a future release.

You should also capture anecdotal information when performing a postmortem analysis. I encourage you to reach out to your editor and publicist for feedback concerning the release. They may have more insight with regard to market and media demands which may have impacted the book's performance.

Upon the conclusion of a postmortem analysis, you may feel the need to share results with an editor, agent, or publicity team. It is imperative that you construct postmortems as useful learning tools, free from emotion or blame. Using the tool to assign blame to a particular group, person, or publisher will only alienate their support on future projects. Sharing results will impress upon the publishing team your dedication to improving relationships and results. It will also serve as a platform for the entire team to make future decisions.

It could be easy to fall into the trap of measuring nearly everything; however, I do not encourage you to do so. Yes, it is important to know what works versus what does not, and I have provided an outline for you to glean such results. Measurement can help you to identify and correct problems as well as provide an analysis to a publisher of the activities. However, to measure accurately and routinely takes time, and this sometimes conflicts with writing. Remember, in your career, the storytelling is always most important. Published books are the largest contributor to your career longevity, and unfortunately, there's no measurement for that. Therefore, measure what you can. And be sure to include your gut reaction for why you believe something isn't working. While there's no measurement for visceral reactions, the author who knows his or her audience, knows best.

Key takeaways from this chapter:

* Effective communication in social media is measured by likes, shares, comments, or retweets of particular posts.

* Measure a target audience by using a survey.

* Measure digital advertising by examining the number of impressions, clicks, click-through rate, cost per click, conversion rate, and cost per action.

* Measure print advertising by number of impressions and redemption rates.

* Measure newsletters by open rate and click-through rate.

* Measure blogs by the number of subscribers, number of comments, number of site/blog hits.

* Measure contests by the goal of the contest.

* Measure reviews by quantity.

* Any press coverage that you did not pay for is a win.

* Measure direct mail by response rate.

* Conversion is the attempt to turn a reader who is "just browsing" into a book buyer.

* Measure your street team via a points-based system or by a system of checks and balances.

* A postmortem analysis is a process which is conducted at the end of a particular project to determine successes and the root cause of failures.

Conclusion

Here, I hope to not only summarize the book but give you, the reader, some of my personal insights from working as a marketer, and now freelance publicist, for over fifteen years. When you engage with this book, don't scan through it merely looking for help with your problem areas, but digest the book as a whole, much like a python having a meal. Read it, think about it, and follow what your gut tells you in order to apply these many marketing theories and methodologies to your career.

In this section, you will find my opinions and advice. Remember, not every piece of advice works for every author. It is important that you don't follow the "herd" mentality. It's false to think that just because a piece of advertising or promotion worked for Tawny Weber or Hank Philippi Ryan, it will work for you. Why won't it? Because of the differences in the wants and needs of each individual readership.

We now know marketing is a discipline that combines strategy, creativity, execution, and most importantly, measurement. Marketing has to be learned and practiced. There are no hard and fast rules to make sure you're doing it right. And that's okay. Why? Because every audience is different. It will take time to perfect what works best for you and your readers.

Needless to say, every author is encouraged to adopt marketing and promotion as part of their career, and make it part of their book launch routine. Without putting effort into marketing, you will find it difficult to find new readers and grow your sales. Therefore, read Chapter One again and practice writing multi-layered messages. Writing using the approach I've outlined may seem awkward at first, but keep trying. Write and revise your messaging. Communicate to the audience what's engaging about the story, make them care. This way you will avoid "screwing up" in social media, and you'll never sound pushy or desperate. You will naturally sound warm and enthusiastic while cultivating an audience who is interested in the book's content.

Does every marketing message have to be multi-layered or begin with a question? No. However, writing marketing messages similar to ad copy is the easiest way for me to teach you how to communicate. I provided a bulleted list to guide you through writing more to your audience than, "Hey, guys, my book is for sale," a message that is sure to get you nowhere, because, deep down, your audience wants to know more. They want to interact with you.

As I've said before, good communication will engage an audience, hook readers, and drive people toward an action, like making a purchase. But, don't stop there.

Take a second look at Chapter Two. During this chapter, think about how wide a reach you can realistically attain before selecting a strategy. If your book has limited distribution, or many people won't find it appealing, mass marketing may not be best suited for you. Think about who you want to find. Does your book have a message that may appeal to more than one group of readers? If so, consider using a differentiated marketing plan. When executing a differentiated marketing plan, the promotional tools (advertising, social media, press coverage, etc.) are the same . . . the message to each, individual audience is what changes.

Will your book only apply to a small, distinct population? If so, niche marketing is your go-to strategy. Keep your promotions tight and focused on one sole buying group. Make sure your messaging is clear and speaks to what your buying group cares about.

Or, maybe you are an author who simply cares about finding readers of a certain genre. If this is you, consider employing a concentrated marketing strategy. With this strategy, you will want to ensure that every promotional tool, dollar of your budget, and social media message targets the readers you want.

As the brilliant Kristen Lamb said, "True discoverability comes when the reader who only reads one to four books a year selects yours."

Which strategy will you use to reach those book buyers?

Mass, differentiated, concentrated, and niche, are marketing strategies which can help you attain a wider readership. If you are only interested in attracting the hard-core romance reader, you'll choose a concentrated marketing strategy. However, keep in mind that when you plateau, it will be time for you to use a different strategy to find more readers; hence, the importance of familiarizing yourself with all of the strategies available to you.

Once you have found your audience, you should begin engagement. Start slow. Create messages to encourage conversation. Talk about books, movies, hobbies and interests, food. In essence, talk about anything to get the dialogue started. Don't be afraid to let your personality show. If you're funny, tell a joke or share a funny image you found online. If you're more serious-minded, talk about real world issues (without being controversial) and share your opinions.

The connection you build brings the audience closer into your world, and the more likely they will be not only to buy your book, but tell others about it as well. Pay special attention to the words you use when communicating to readers. Ask rather than tell. If you feel a message you are creating for social media sounds too pushy, try rewriting the message three times. Use the third version.

Authors have often asked me if it's possible to "screw up" in social media. Yes, it is. Mistakes often happen because the author doesn't know how to conduct him or herself online. Avoid controversial topics. That should be fairly simple advice to remember. I mean, would you buy something from someone who made you angry? No.

Also, even if you hate marketing and promotion, don't tell your audience. One of the worst tweets I've ever read went something like this, "I hate promotion. Please buy my book so I don't have to do it anymore." Then, the author pasted her buy link in the tweet. Now, let me ask you. After reading this tweet, would you buy the book?

Probably not. Not only does it sound lazy, but it's also an example of a hard-sell message. There is no engaging content. Plus, it makes the author sound desperate, and people tend to avoid desperate people. Think of social media communication like this: if you wouldn't say it to someone's face, don't say it online. That rule should help you keep from screwing up online.

I also talk about brand in detail in Chapter Three. Why? Because establishing who you are is the number one most essential building block of marketing and promotion. As an author, you have to be able to communicate who you are and what you are about. It is that simple.

I cannot stress enough how important authenticity is to your brand. *Be your brand* is not a cliché. It is integral to sustainability and success in this business. If you cannot put a stake in the ground to say this is who I am and what I'm about, how do you expect the reader to know?

The worst thing that can possibly happen is for a reader to say, "I read a good story, but I can't remember the title or who wrote it." And, believe me, that's what readers will say if your brand is not established. Well-crafted brand statements let the reader know what to expect before they begin reading. Brand statements also assist buyers who are on the fence make a judgment about whether or not they would like to try your book.

I want to talk to the pre-published authors for a moment.

For aspiring authors, creating a brand is just as important as it is for published authors. Whether you choose to independently publish or seek publication through more traditional channels, establishing a brand prior to publication shows the prospective agent, editor, and reader that you have an understanding of marketing, which most commonly begins with brand building.

If you are already established, endorsements by fellow authors in your same genre can assist in building your brand.

Published authors sometimes ask me if endorsements on book covers sell books. Unfortunately, I have no data to support the answer to this question positively or negatively. However, having an endorsement from a fellow author or subject matter expert, if you write nonfiction, can help a reader make a decision to try someone new. Please don't be shy in asking for an endorsement. Follow the tips listed in Chapter Three should you need guidance. Remember, an author endorsement helps to build credibility among readers. In the reader's mind, it is logical for them to think, "Oh, this author liked it. I like this author, so maybe I'll like this new one, too." And, that connection is all you are hoping for.

Endorsements are great. But when it comes to publishing, what name do you choose? Given name or pen name?

If you decide to build a brand around a pen name, that's no problem. Chapter Four provides tips for creating a pen name. Many authors choose to use pen names for various reasons. Using a pen name or publishing under your given name is an individual choice. However, some authors may think that the more names, the wider the audience and therefore additional sales for their entire body of work is generated. This isn't so. Should you choose to publish under more than one name, there may be some audience/reader crossover, but it is not guaranteed, especially if you are publishing in a different genre.

Remember, for each pen name you create, you should establish a brand to help support the name. Is publishing under a pen name like starting over with audience building? Yes. However, some authors thrive under more than one name. Take a look at Kate Locke or Jayne Ann Krentz, if you need examples.

However, if you find using a pen name doesn't work for you, take a lesson from Jessica Andersen, and examine her efforts in blending her two audiences. It truly doesn't matter what name you use, as long as you build a healthy brand to support it.

Remember, be your brand. Always.

Chapter Five discusses how building a strong, relatable brand can help you if you encounter a public relations crisis. I'm certain anyone in this industry can think of an instance of an author flame-out or meltdown. I know I can remember a time when an author should've known when to be quiet, but didn't until it was too late. Mistakes in the public eye can happen. Press misprints or a social media meltdown can cause an upheaval. Controversial or negative opinions on blogs can cause a mini-crisis, especially in an industry that remains as in flux as the publishing industry.

Remember to be strong and handle these crises professionally.

Having a solidly built brand can help you with weathering storms. Therefore, I urge you to do the work in setting up alerts and notifications. It doesn't matter what site you use. It is more important to have a notification mechanism in place so that you aren't blindsided if something is said about you online.

If the issue is due to a misprint in the media, address the mishap truthfully with your readership and work to spin the news to your advantage. Tips on how to help you manage a media crisis are found in Chapter Five. If you find yourself the subject of a scathing or negative review, do not engage or respond to the reader or professional reviewer. It's vital that you remain calm and don't lose your cool.

I created the acronym ACORN. Maybe it will stick in your mind and you will remember what to do before the temptation of engaging in negative behavior online strikes. Let's review it one more time to make sure you remember all of the important points.

A stands for Acknowledge. If you learn something negative exists about you online or is reported in the media and it requires a response (remember, not all remarks do), communicate that you are saddened by the event and are working to repair the situation.

C stands for Communicate. Should you find yourself in crisis, don't disappear. Refrain from acting like an ostrich with your head in the sand. Crises call for professionalism and responsiveness. If you need help from your editor, agent, publicist, or fellow authors, ask for it.

O stands for Offer assistance. If it is within your control, you may want to consider offering assistance in helping to rectify a situation.

R stands for Remain professional. Yes, I know this can be hard. As authors, we treat our books like our children, but we also need to realize as we send our children out into the world to face whatever may come, we do the same with our books. Walk away. Take a breath. And realize that acting rashly will only come back to damage your brand.

N stands for Never engage. Don't start the disagreement. You and I will always encounter people who rub us the wrong way. There will always be the blogger who thinks her opinion is more valued than others, or the unsatisfied reader who didn't get what they wanted no matter how hard you tried. Let it go. It is easier said than done, I know. I've been there. Always keep your long-term goals and aspirations in the front of your mind. Remember what's at stake long-term. This is your career.

Chapter Six takes an in-depth look at one way you can grow your readership by striving to cultivate a fan base. If we worked in corporate America, we would call these people brand loyalists. But, as authors, we refer to these mega-readers as "super fans." Finding the super fan is like finding a diamond in the rough, pardon the cliché, but these people can help you build your brand, spread the word about your books, and help you find new readers for little other reason than they love your work.

One technique you can use to find such fans is by employing the use of the AIDA model. This model is over one hundred years old and it has lasted the test of time. AIDA means Attention, Interest, Desire, and Action. These are the basic steps you need to take in driving, not only awareness of your book, but the purchase as well. Over the years, AIDA has been examined, and is now modernized to reflect the changes in consumer communications, opinions, and loyalties.

If you really get into this stuff, as I do, I highly recommend you read the paper entitled, "The Development of The Hierarchy of Effects Model in Advertising," by Bambang Sukma Wijaya in its entirety. It is published in the *International Journal of Research Business Studies* and can be found online.

The brilliance behind the AISDALSLove (attention, interest, search, desire, action, like, share, and love) is its expansion of the AIDA model. It provides a modern-day approach to helping you identify your super fans by learning the steps of the model and then assigning promotional tools to support each phase of the process.

Chapter Six provides some examples of promotional tools that may be beneficial to use in each stage. For example, to support a reader in their search, make sure you have listed all links, info, blurbs, metadata, and keywords online to help the reader find your book.

Also, I'd like to point out in Chapter Six that, although I received permission to reprint data from RWA and Sisters in Crime regarding reader demographics and buying patterns, organizations such as these routinely provide this type of information to their members. Use this information to your advantage to market smart.

Here's what I mean. If we know that sixty-eight percent of mystery buyers are female and thirty-five percent of mystery buyers live in the South (as reported by Sisters in Crime) use this knowledge to target your digital advertising to mystery-reading females who live in the South. Data exists. Take the time to understand it and use it to its full advantage. Once you've succeeded in cultivating your fan base, remember to reward their loyalty with unputdownable reads.

Additionally, performing the strategy tool exercises prior to jumping into promotion will help you to wisely spend your marketing budget, learn what the target audience expects, and help you justify saying, "no, thank you." Why? Because promotional opportunities may arise and you will question whether or not you should participate; if you know where you're lacking, the decision will be easier to make.

Therefore, I strongly urge you to consult Chapter Seven to work though the strategy tools. Crafting a position statement will detail what you expect to deliver to the reader with every release. It is an exercise that may sound fluffy. I assure you it is not. After you write your statement, post it near your workstation. Keep it close as an affirmation of who you are really working for (the reader) and what they expect.

A multi-use tool that can be very advantageous is a SWOT analysis. The SWOT analysis is a powerful tool to understand one's strengths, weaknesses, opportunities, and threats. Because it's a comprehensive tool, performing a SWOT analysis for planning, brainstorming, or decision-making can be particularly useful. Couple the SWOT analysis with the author landscape analysis to identify where you may be falling behind in your promotions or if you are ahead of the curve.

For the purpose of this analysis, stick to monitoring the promotional activities performed by yourself and your peers. At the very least, bring yourself up to par with those similar to you in your genre. The results of this analysis will identify gaps in your marketing activity which you must work to improve upon.

Once you've identified where you need to make improvements, you will need to assign a budget to bring about changes needed to your promotional activity. Chapter Eight provides you with examples. My personal rule of thumb for building a budget is to research all of your costs, add them, and include an additional twenty percent into the budget for hidden "gotchas." Chapter Eight walked you through what putting a budget together might look like. If you have extra money you would like to spend on marketing, invest in activities which will lend themselves toward discoverability. Invest in making sure people know who you are.

You may find that a big line item in your budget is devoted to a publicist. Yes, freelance publicists are expensive. Publicists do not do the same kind of work as an assistant does. Before choosing to hire a publicist, make sure you are really in need of what they have to offer.

If you need help with the media, branding, making industry contacts, or career guidance, a publicist may be able to assist. I encourage you to vet anyone to whom you are giving your hard-earned money. Ask for a list of clients who would be willing to be contacted, and perform the due diligence needed to make sure your needs are matched to a publicist who works within your genre.

In a healthy publicist/author relationship, you should feel as though you have an advocate who is invested in your success. If you do not, I encourage you to reevaluate your relationship with your publicist. Personally speaking, during my many years as a freelance publicist, there have been many clients with whom I "click" with very well. To me, these clients seem more like friends, and I will not hesitate to go out of my way to help them. However, not all clients are created equal. I have had my share of high-maintenance, demanding clients. These relationships resulted in my deleting them from my business. Treat your relationship with your publicist as a special one. If your publicist is not spending time with you to develop plans for the future, you should probably seek out a new relationship.

If you do not have the money to hire a freelance publicist, don't worry. This book is designed so that won't need one. My goal in writing *Market or Die* is to equip you with the tools needed to execute your own marketing plan. So, remember, when doing your own publicity, focus on discoverability and getting your name "out there" and not solely on sales. Networking with authors and industry personnel within your genre is the perfect way to begin creating buzz for your brand.

What I enjoyed about writing this book is that it allowed for separate discussions about marketing strategy and execution. Chapter Nine put both elements together. Remember the gaps we talked about during the Author Landscape Analysis. Chapter Nine explained the pros and cons for the promotional tools used to fill those gaps. For example, if you are having a discoverability problem, consider using a mix of advertising and promoted social media posts to bring awareness to your book. Book reviews also help readers discover new authors. It is imperative that you assign promotional tools to fill the gaps. Why? If you leave the holes in your marketing plan "as is," these gaps will only grow over time. If you leave these "unfilled holes" unattended, one day you will realize that you are too far behind with your promotions and it will be impossible to catch up to the market without a significant investment in both time and money.

All of your promotional activities should be designed to build your network. And, when I say build your network, I am speaking about the entire community of readers, fellow authors, and publication industry professionals within your reach. Your network and your "sphere of influence" are essentially the same thing. Just as some personal relationships are closer than others, so are professional and industry relationships. That feeling of closeness is dissected in order to describe the core, inner, and outer circles in Chapter Ten.

Through all of our efforts with networking and audience-building, the goal should be to bring those people from your outer circle into your inner circle. And, as the inner circle grows, so will the outer circle, essentially widening your presence within the marketplace. If you take a conscious approach to building your network, it will help you stay relevant in the marketplace. Why? Because you will be in the know of what readers and industry personnel are looking for.

One way to help keep yourself informed and connected with your readership is by using social media. In Chapter Eleven, Kristen Lamb contributed (and thankfully she agreed to do so) to this section because I value her opinion. I knew she would give my readers the answers to the "what." What do authors need to know about social media? What are the pros and cons? What are the advantages of blogging? I wanted her to answer this and many other questions because of her proficiency and expertise in social media.

Sure, I know about social media and what makes social media work for authors, but my forte is marketing strategy. I get excited figuring out and then explaining the "why." Why is this author having difficulty finding an audience? Why can't an author connect with his or her readership? Etc. Therefore, I hope you find Chapter Eleven helpful, because I have taken Kristen's explanation of the *what* and paired her answers with the pros and cons of the *why*. This way, you can not only ask what social media platform is right for you, but why you should use it.

Using social media is a powerful tool to help you in creating mindshare. As explained in Chapter Twelve, mindshare focuses on the quantity and frequency a consumer thinks about a brand. Your goal is to incorporate emotion into your brand and make it memorable.

For fun, let's test your mindshare. Think about the name of your favorite book or its author. Can you picture the cover? Can you visualize him or her? Can you name the last book you read by this person? If you can do all of those things, this person has built mindshare within you.

So, were you successful with this exercise? I was. While I have many favorite authors, one of my absolute favorites is Stephen King. The book cover that came to mind was the cover of *Under the Dome*. I pictured Mr. King in my mind. The photo was one of the black and white images from his website. Actually it's one of the few pictures of him without glasses. And the last book I read by him was *Doctor Sleep*. Because my brain can recall all of this simply by me asking myself to think of a favorite author, that tells me that Mr. King's brand has created mindshare within my brain. His work (I've never met him personally) has left such a strong impression on me that I not only can recall everything about it, but his brand conjures a chilling feeling of excitement in me because I can recall exactly how I feel when I am reading one of his books.

Now that's powerful stuff.

And the cool part? All authors have the power to create mindshare. If you're in doubt that you can indeed create mindshare among your readership, go back and review Chapter Twelve. Watch the videos recommended in this chapter because these videos are a good, visual example of the emotion the brand has created, and the delivery of the emotion to the viewer. If you don't remember anything else about mindshare, remember this: mindshare mixes brand with emotion.

One topic we all have emotions about (and probably not positive ones) is measurement and sustainability. Dry, boring, heavily time-consuming and, ah, yes, a necessary evil, building mechanisms for measurement into your marketing plan is inherent to your job. Why? Because since authors have now become the CEOs of our own small businesses, you and I must take a vested interest in what marketing efforts work for us and which ones do not. For example, knowing where you excel, such as what times of the year work best for certain promotions, if your newsletter database is growing and if the newsletter is being read, how often and by whom, are all important pieces of information for you to know in order to grow.

It is vital that you routinely review your website metrics. Who is visiting your site? How long do they stay? What are they clicking on? If you have a website, you must capture these analytics. Do you have to use Google Analytics? No. Use a reporting system you understand and are comfortable with. In Chapter Thirteen, I have listed some very easy metrics for you to use to begin your evaluations.

"But I don't have the time."

If I've heard this excuse once, I've heard it a thousand times. If you are serious about growing your readership, selling more copies of books, and penetrating the marketplace to get your name in front of a vast majority of readers, you must make time. So, suck it up, Buttercup, and read Chapter Thirteen until you become comfortable with metrics.

As your teacher, I didn't put anything in this book you can't handle. It's easy to shy away from measurement. Unlike your book, there is no editor hovering over your shoulder to make sure you get measuring done. Right?

Wrong.

If this is your first time experimenting with metrics, here's what I'd like you to do:

* Collect three months' worth of data.

* Record it (preferably in Excel).

* Send me an email with your data attached to jenniferafusco@gmail.com and I will help you with interpreting your results.

If you are an experienced author who measures your activity routinely, you are moving in the right direction. Congratulations. However, I'd like to ask you to stretch yourself. Try performing a postmortem analysis. Email your completed analysis to me at the address above and let's discuss it together. Using a postmortem analysis will help you identify where your plan went "off the rails." If you are asked by an editor or agent to explain why something happened, this is an excellent tool to use for pointing out cause and effect.

Beginning a postmortem may seem, at first, like you are simply assigning blame or drumming up excuses for why a promotional effort didn't work. If, at the end of your analysis, it reads like a "blame game," it's time to go deeper. Always support your claims with facts. Use numbers. Revisit your metrics with a critical eye and pinpoint the exact moment during your plan's momentum where your wheels fell off. The postmortem analysis isn't designed to make you feel discouraged or angry. If these feelings arise during your examination, set the analysis aside and allow more time to pass before returning to it. Remember, emotion during analysis clouds judgment. And it is our aim to use the results of a postmortem for future decision-making, budgeting, and goal planning.

Give it a try. You may just amaze yourself with what you uncover.

Marketing and the Future

I'm asked a lot about where I see the future of author marketing going. I believe we can look to what is happening with television, films, and to some degree, in corporate America to use as our crystal ball. So, I see future changes happening for us much like this: If you, as the consumer, enjoy a particular experience, be it through a book, movie, television show, or engagement with a product, the goal of their marketing will be to deliver these same experiences repeatedly so that you will engage with the brand as long as possible.

In my opinion, we saw this happen organically with the Stephenie Meyer's Twilight Saga. First, there were the books. And, regardless of your opinion of the books themselves, no one can argue that they weren't successful sellers. They were tremendous bestsellers. But, for fans, the series wasn't enough. So when Hollywood came calling, this was great for fans of the series. There, the fans got to relive the experience of the books through the movies all over again. But, their craving for everything *Twilight* didn't stop there. Avid fans sought out in-person tours of the areas within Washington and Canada where the book was either mentioned or the places were used in the filming of the movies. Merchandising went crazy. During the success of the books and films, we saw everything from *Twilight* clothing to lunchboxes. Fans hosted *Twilight*-themed parties. And, they kept the love of the world in motion straight through the release of the DVDs.

In essence, the readers didn't want to let go of the world created in *Twilight*, and they actively sought out more and more opportunities in which to immerse themselves.

There is a marketing term to support this behavior. It's called experiential marketing. Experiential marketing uses all five senses to engage a consumer with a product, and engage them repeatedly. Experiential marketing allows a brand to essentially come alive.

Going forward, for all writers, the question will become, not how do I market my book, but how can the reader fully experience the book? How many senses can I draw upon to bring the reader closer to the world created by the book?

Now, not all writers are going to have Hollywood knocking on their doors. If you've worked in this business long enough, you understand that. But that doesn't mean you can't take some steps to immerse the reader in the book's world, and keep them there for as long as you can.

Let's brainstorm how we can begin to accomplish this.

For example, let's create a character who cooks. A man. A hot, sexy man. Maybe he's an executive chef, and you think it'd be a great idea to list the recipes our hero chef creates in the book. So, they are listed in the back for the readers, so they can make the dishes themselves. Super. We see this all the time in cozy mysteries.

But what else could we, as the author, do to immerse the reader and draw them into the world of our handsome chef? Maybe it's an in-person cooking contest sponsored by the author (and our handsome hero, of course). Maybe the author hosts (in addition to a book signing) a taste test of all of the different recipes in the book. Maybe the author takes her fans on a restaurant kitchen tour. Or, maybe the author creates a virtual kitchen on her website which allows readers to submit their photos of the dishes they've made from the book.

The possibilities are endless.

Your goal with experiential marketing is to keep the reader immersed in the world of the book using multiple and varied experiences (and incorporating all of the five senses) for as long as possible.

Need more real-life examples to fully understand the concept? Okay. Here we go.

Have you ever heard of Tide laundry detergent? Yes. Well, Tide is coming off the shelf in your laundry room and into a metro area near you with the franchised extension of their brand, Tide Dry Cleaners. Here, customers are met with the same brand loyalty built with products they've used inside their homes and they are taking that loyalty outside the home for their dry cleaning needs. As a marketer, the goal is that when a consumer has a need for clothes cleaning, they automatically think about Tide.

Many corporations are slowly transforming their brand into something more tangible. And, good heavens, if corporate America can do it, we certainly can. Making a brand tangible allows the consumer to become fully engaged. This engagement builds the brand, mindshare, and sets the stage for repeat purchases.

If you want to experience this type of marketing firsthand, walk into your local Starbucks. Starbucks, a company at the forefront of marketing, has used experiential marketing for years. The company has made a visit to Starbucks unlike a visit anyplace else.

If you have visited Starbucks, you know as soon as you walk inside you're going to be hit with what? The smell. Roasted coffee beans. Mmmm. Then, you go and wait in line, and admire all the pastries which are a visual treat. Eclectic music plays while you wait, giving your ears a delight and your brain something to subconsciously process. Then, you move to the counter where you order your coffee using Starbucks' own special lingo. And, after you're served, you move to one of their comfy sofas and chairs to enjoy your purchase.

This, my friends, is a full sensory experience.

Starbucks has created an environment, a world, where the consumer will want to spend a great deal of their time, and are eager to return. They deliver their brand promise in that every visit to Starbucks, no matter the location, is exactly the same. The consumer knows what to expect and experience.

Starbucks' marketing and brand management is top-notch. It is a company we can learn from.

Like everything in marketing and promotion, it's important that if you choose to experiment with experiential marketing, you make the experience for the reader both memorable and interactive. Challenge yourself to deliver an experience that will draw the reader closer to your characters and your books. By doing this, you will unconsciously draw readers closer to you and your brand. There, you can build upon the relationship you make with your readers for years to come.

Thank You

You did it! Here's the part in the book where I want you to pat yourself on the back for hanging in there with me to help you become the best marketer you can be. Getting to this point wasn't easy. And, you may still have some unanswered questions. If at any time you want to drop me a line with a question or if you need further information, feel free to send an email to: jenniferafusco@gmail.com. I'll respond as soon as I can.

I hope you found this book informative. If you found it helpful, I would like to encourage you to leave a review online and mention this book to your fellow writers. Help me spread the word about *Market or Die* on social media, especially to those who have trouble with marketing. There is light at the end of the tunnel. If you are committed to a writing career,

I know you'll become a fantastic marketer. You can do it. Hang in there. Refer back to the chapters when you feel stuck, and don't be afraid to try something new. Your future readers will thank you.

Acknowledgements

I would like to extend a very heartfelt note of thanks to the wonderful authors, educators, and professional industry contacts that provided permissions, quotes, interviews, or examples for this book. Your wisdom is truly inspiring.

(in alphabetical order)

Jessica Andersen, Kim Boykin

Loretta Chase, Michael Clark

Dani Collins, Cynthia D'Alba

Matthew Doss, Ted Fauster

Kate George, Molly Harper

Gwen Hayes, Sara Humphreys

Lori Handeland, Kristan Higgins

Eloisa James, Suzanne Johnson

Kristen Lamb, RM Lane

Katy Lee, A.M. Madden

Nicole Resciniti, Hank Phillippi Ryan

Kate Smith, Anton Strout

Barbara Vey, Tawny Weber

Sarah Wendell

Professor Bambang Wijaya, Bakrie University, Jakarta

About the Author

Photo Credit: Mark Borderud

Jennifer Fusco is the owner of Market or Die, a publicity services company.

A three-time winner of the Advertising Excellence Award, Jennifer has launched successful national print and digital ad campaigns. She has served as a member of the Association of National Advertisers (ANA) and believes brand-building is a key to professional success.

In her writing life, Ms. Fusco writes contemporary romance for Penguin Group. Her first book, *Fighting for It*, will debut in September 2015. She is also a bi-monthly contributor to the Romance Writers of America's *Romance Writers Report*.

See more at: marketordie.net

22052312R00117

Made in the USA
Middletown, DE
18 July 2015